Practical Solutions for Stabilizing Students With Classic Autism to Be Ready to Learn

Practical Solutions for Stabilizing Students With Classic Autism to Be Ready to Learn

Getting to Go!

Judy Endow, MSW

Foreword by Brenda Smith Myles, Ph.D.

PUBLISHING

© 2011 AAPC
P.O. Box 23173
Shawnee Mission, Kansas 66283-0173
www.asperger.net

Publisher's Cataloging-in-Publication

Endow, Judy.

Practical solutions for stabilizing students with classic autism to be ready to learn : getting to go! / Judy Endow ; foreword by Brenda Smith Myles. -- Shawnee Mission, Kan. : Autism Asperger Pub. Co., c2010.

  p. ; cm.

  ISBN: 978-1-934575-75-8
  LCCN: 2010934912
  Includes bibliographical references.

    1. Autistic children--Education--Study and teaching. 2. Autistic children--Behavior modification. 3. Autism spectrum disorders--Treatment. 4. Sensory integration dysfunction in children--Treatment. 5. Self-control in children--Study and teaching.
  6. Teachers of children with disabilities--Handbooks, manuals, etc.
  I. Title.

RJ506.A9 E53 2010
618.92/85882--dc22   1009

This book is designed in Helvetica Neue and Impact.

Printed in the United States of America.

For all the Devans in the world

and all those who love and support them ...

That they may start on their journey

to becoming all they were meant to be

and all they may want to be

as they grow up into adulthood.

Courtesy Rori Daams

Devan is a remarkable boy I've had the pleasure of working with for the past few years. All of Devan's team members have been successfully trained in the strategies outlined in this book, as have the teams of countless other children like Devan.

Table of Contents

Foreword

Judy Endow first talked with me about the concept for this book when she was at my home for a visit. I listened with great interest as she explained what she does when supporting individuals with autism in schools, homes, and communities. She talked about self-regulation, an area that I have been passionate about, but she did so in a different way than it is typically practiced. Specifically, in order to provide effective supports to the learner with ASD, she first stabilizes him. She ensures that the learner's system is regulated (or organized) and then provides information in her first language – visual. This allows her to begin to understand what the learner needs to take in, process, learn, and apply. Before anyone can learn, he or she must be in a "ready to learn" mode. This includes being regulated and knowing that a structure exists in one's first language. Simple – yet brilliant!

This book is replete with information that will help individuals meet their potential. One of the underlying constructs here and, indeed, in everything Judy does is "person-first attitude" (Endow, personal communication, June 27, 2010). We are all familiar with the concept of "person-first language" – talking about the person before referencing her exceptionality (i.e., a "child with autism" instead of the "autistic child"). "Person-first attitude," according to Judy, is what some of us get after using "person-first language." Unlike "person-first language," it cannot be mandated. "Person-first attitude" is not about how we use the power of our words to benefit people with disabilities. Instead, "person-first attitude" is a reflection of what we become while in relationship with each other. It is the elusive substance of how our hearts respond to our common humanity rather than the correctness of our language in response to their disability.

I am honored to write this brief introduction. Judy has taught me so much professionally and personally. I am glad that we are friends. To the reader, I hope you enjoy and learn from this very important book.

P.S. Judy treats me with person-first attitude also!

– Brenda Smith Myles, Ph.D., a consultant with the Ziggurat Group, is the recipient of the 2004 Autism Society of America's Outstanding Professional Award and the 2006 Princeton Fellowship Award. She has written numerous articles and books on Asperger Syndrome and autism, including *Asperger Syndrome and Difficult Moments: Practical Solutions for Tantrums, Rage, and Meltdowns* (with Southwick) and *Asperger Syndrome and Adolescence: Practical Solutions for School Success* (with Adreon). The latter is the winner of the Autism Society of America's 2002 Outstanding Literary Work.

Introduction

To ensure the best possible outcomes for individuals with an autism spectrum disorder (ASD), proactive supports must be in place. From the moment of initial diagnosis, whether it is pervasive developmental disorder-not otherwise specified (PDD-NOS), classic autism, or Asperger Syndrome (AS), it would be wonderful if everyone were assessed using a comprehensive model of assessment, support, and intervention. Sadly, this is still far from the norm, even though it is entirely possible at this point in the history of autism by employing such tools as The Ziggurat Model (Aspy & Grossman, 2008) and the Comprehensive Autism Planning System (CAPS) (Henry & Myles, 2007).

It is this reality in our schools and other settings that drives the need for this book. Even though we have the methodology to deliver proactive assessment, support, and intervention, we do not have a consistent systems structure with adequately trained personnel to do so for all students with ASD. As a result, we remain largely in a reactive mode. In fact, the modus operandi in our school systems seems to be that if students are not exhibiting behavior that we find challenging, we pretty much assume they are doing okay. This is especially so when students are getting average or better grades. When students with ASD with the most significant challenges exhibit extreme behavior in an educational setting, of necessity, we adopt a reactive stance. If a student has extreme or aggressive behaviors, we must do something, especially if he is hurting self or others or if his behavior has potential to do so.

My hope is that as more of us in the field come to know better, we will figure out a way to do better within the systems in which we work. In the meantime, we must have a strategy to put in place immediately to decrease the occurrence of extreme behaviors.

This book addresses that need. Specifically, as an autism consultant, I have found that by putting in place an interactive visual schedule along with a "sensory diet" (Wilbarger, 1995) as a first step, much of everything else, including behaviors, sorts out with the kids with classic autism. It cuts to the chase of needing to put in lots of other things. This book presents practical strategies to stabilize the student with classic autism through those two avenues.

The order of the book will follow the structure I use in sorting out the situations I walk into during the course of my everyday work; namely,

- **supporting internal organization/regulation with sensory strategies, and**
- **supporting external organization/regulation with a visual schedule.**

 An extra bonus is that the strategies as outlined in this book, when applied to a child with classic autism who is not exhibiting extreme or explosive behaviors, pave the way for the child to be all he can be; that is, his best version of self and most available for learning. The information presented here has been used throughout my practice as an autism consultant and has become many children's ticket onward – to eventually be placed in an inclusive educational setting.

When to Use the Strategies in This Book

A functional behavior assessment (FBA) is often done for children with extreme or aggressive behaviors. While waiting for the FBA, readers can use the information in this book to help stabilize the child's behavior. For many students I have worked with, once these stabilization interventions have been put in place, a significant reduction in the behavior of concern occurs. In some cases, the behavior even disappears! When this happens, people might assume that the problem has been solved and that, therefore, the FBA is no longer necessary. While it is true that current difficult behavior may no longer be evident, if the underlying autism is not supported, new behaviors will likely emerge. So, it is important to not stop here!

Introduction

In other words, rather than providing all the answers, this book offers an immediate pick-up-and-use strategy for pre-FBA stabilization. From there the student is best served by a team assessment from which a plan of support and intervention is developed to address the student's underlying characteristics of autism.

 My personal preference is to use the Ziggurat Model (Aspy & Grossman, 2008) for this sort of assessment, support, and intervention. It is a comprehensive FBA tool that goes far beyond the stabilization strategies offered in this book. It is recommended that the Ziggurat Model be used along with CAPS (*The Comprehensive Autism Planning System*; Henry & Myles, 2007), which shows how to imbed the support strategies into the student's daily schedule.

The pre-FBA stabilization strategies may be thought of in terms of medical stabilization of patients before they undergo treatment for an underlying disease. Just like medical stabilization will not address the underlying medical disease, neither will pre-FBA stabilization address the underlying autism (Aspy, personal communication, 2009). Why anyone would choose to offer a student stabilization and then never provide support for the underlying autism is hard for me to understand, yet I know it is sometimes so.

The stabilization affords students better regulated bodies. As students become better regulated and better able to communicate effectively, extreme behaviors decrease, sometimes subsiding altogether. Once regulated and ready to "go," so to speak, the behaviors these students have left can be further sorted out by using an FBA – the usual starting place for those with the Asperger Syndrome (AS) or high-functioning autism (HFA) who are engaging in behaviors that do not serve them well. But if the FBA is used as the starting place for students with classic autism, it has variable results, and most often leaves us with the feeling that we are just spinning our wheels in that we rarely seem to get anywhere significant.

In this era of recognizing the benefits of inclusive classrooms (Kluth, 2003), far too many students with classic autism remain segregated from the general student population. I believe that in lots of cases this is due more to their displays of behavior that disrupt the learning environment for the rest of the students than it is due to their actual learning needs.

Although many students have made it out of the segregated special education classroom, students with the trickiest neurologies – those with classic autism – are still often found in a classroom with a few other special needs students and sometimes in their very own classroom of one, an island unto themselves in the midst of a school full of their peers. In other instances, these students have an abbreviated school day, some attending school for as little as 30-40 minutes each day.

So that more students with classic autism will find a greater degree of success and ultimately be afforded the opportunity of an inclusive education, I have written this book. Although it does not, by itself, allow you to provide a comprehensive intervention plan such as afforded by the Ziggurat Model (Aspy & Grossman, 2008), it will allow for initial stabilization of your student with classic autism – an important beginning.

 The terms *organization* and *regulation* are used interchangeably in this book. Further, the term *sensory modulation* is often used by OTs to refer to internal/sensory regulation.

Chapter 1
Starting Points

The saying "If you have met one person with autism, you have met one person with autism" is absolutely true. I have met many individuals with autism spectrum disorders (ASD) and have yet to find any duplicates. But even though no two people on the autism spectrum are alike, I have found myself making a practical sort into one of two categories when I first begin working with a student. These two categories closely resemble the classic presentation of autism and the Asperger Syndrome (AS) (or high-functioning; HFA) presentation of autism.

The practicality of this sort in the context of the world at large with all the neurotypicals reminds me of a board game. Here is a poem I wrote recently that explains the situation as I see it.

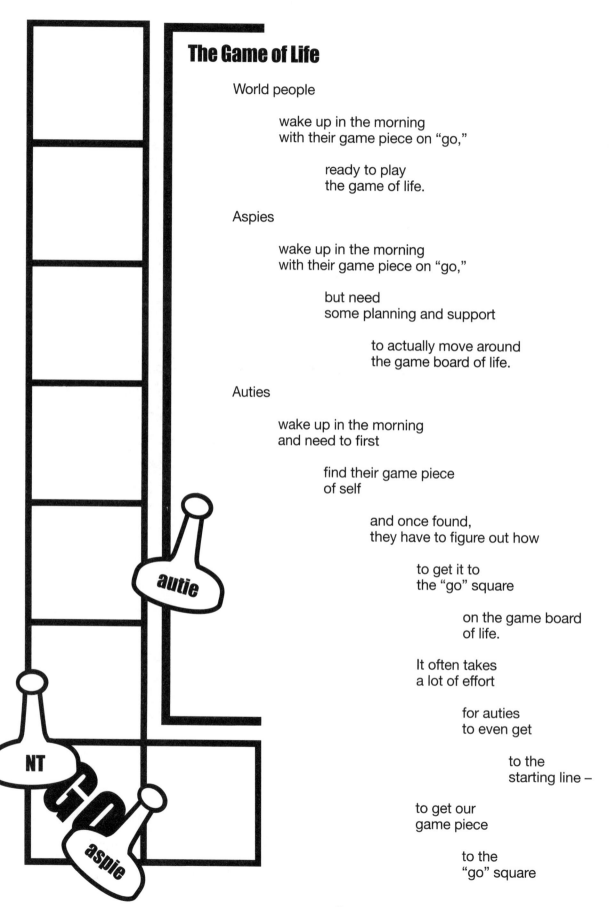

The Game of Life

World people

wake up in the morning
with their game piece on "go,"

ready to play
the game of life.

Aspies

wake up in the morning
with their game piece on "go,"

but need
some planning and support

to actually move around
the game board of life.

Auties

wake up in the morning
and need to first

find their game piece
of self

and once found,
they have to figure out how

to get it to
the "go" square

on the game board
of life.

It often takes
a lot of effort

for auties
to even get

to the
starting line –

to get our
game piece

to the
"go" square

Starting Points

in our game
of life,

but when we do
get to "go,"

we too
then need

some planning
and support

to
actually

move
around

the
game board

of daily
life.

World people, Aspies, and auties

can all play
in the Game of Life

with supports in place
so we all can be

everything
we were meant to be

where each one

"as is"

can belong,

each one having
our spot in the world

where each one

as is
and with
supports in place

can contribute from.

Note: Because I am autistic, I can use the terms of endearment of my autism community to describe my co-horts on the autism spectrum – autie for those with classic autism and Aspie for those with Asperger Syndrome or high-functioning autism. These terms, while terms of endearment when used "by us, for us, and about us by us," are usually not terms the general public should feel free to use when speaking about us.

It is the initial classic autism difference that this book will address to give those in support roles the tools for intervention that will allow those of us with classic autism to get to "Go" in our Game of Life.

Once the student with classic autism is on "Go," the strategies that are helpful for AS/HFA can be employed to maintain optimal game play throughout the day. Sometimes the game piece of the person with classic autism falls off the game board, such as when the sensory system becomes overwhelmed or shuts down. When this happens, we must get the game piece back on the board before proceeding to use the general AS/HFA supports that also work well with those with classic autism when their game piece is in play.

In fact, the strategies put forth in the popular book *Simple Strategies That Work! Helpful Hints for All Educators of Students With Asperger Syndrome, High-Functioning Autism, and Related Disabilities* (Myles, Adreon, & Gitlitz, 2006) are useful for all of us on the spectrum to get through daily life being the best we can be. It is just that those with classic autism among us need to first get to "Go" in order for the strategies to reap the biggest bang for their buck so to speak.

Functional behavioral analyses (FBAs) and behavioral intervention plans (BIPs) are great, but if we employ some preliminary stabilization techniques that support our students with classic autism to find their game piece and to place it on "Go," many of their problematic behaviors disappear. Once having gotten to "Go," if troubling behaviors are still present, a more formal FBA can help us figure out the remaining behavior, subsequently constructing a BIP to positively impact the behavior. If the remaining behavior is escalating, it can be mapped out and proactively addressed, and, in most cases, prevented by using a curriculum such as *Outsmarting Explosive Behavior, A Visual System of Support and Intervention for Individuals with Autism Spectrum Disorders* (Endow, 2009).

For students who do not demonstrate extreme behaviors, this simple system greatly improves their chances of being able to relate, attend, and learn. It doesn't have a fancy name but has served me and my students well. I think of it simply in the Game of Life analogy as "getting to Go;" hence, the name of this book.

 As a person with autism, I have found this to work so well that I use the same system each day in my own life! It allows me to move about in the world in a comfortable manner, employed, engaging with friends, and generally living my day-to-day life being the best version of myself; that is, my well-regulated self.

Chapter 2

A Positive Beginning to Behavior We Find Challenging

A Familiar Scenario

In my work as an autism consultant, I am most often called into a school because a student on the autism spectrum is displaying behavior that is not working well in the classroom environment. For example, the student is trying to push classmates who get too close to him or engages in repetitive behaviors such as hissing or loudly repeating cartoon sound effects and phrases that become distracting to his classmates.

Some of our students display such severe behaviors that staff members are afraid to be alone with them. These students may bang their heads enough to cause concussions, scream for a prolonged time, or hit, bite, kick, throw their bodies, or gouge self or others with enough force to cause bodily harm. Faced with such extreme behavior, staff is often afraid of these students – for their own safety and that of other students in the room.

Because our own survival instinct is triggered by the child's behavior, if we do not understand what is happening, we are likely to blame the child, because intuitively we know that the child's behavior set off our response. As a result, instead of merely saying that the child's behavior triggered our survival response, we end up blaming the child for exhibiting the extreme behavior.

The end result of our own fight/flight response is to come up with ways to NOT be around the student. As mentioned, this often translates into a quite abbreviated school day for the student. This is generally couched in terms of what is best for the student as it is "obvious" that it is the student who cannot handle a full school day as evidenced by the exhibited behaviors.

If you have been or are currently in this kind of situation, first of all, know that your response, given the situation, is reasonable. And now that you have found this book, breathe easier because you will learn strategies that can positively impact your situation.

The Game of Life Analogy

For individuals with AS or HFA who wake up in the morning with their game piece on the "Go" square, ready to play the game of life, this first step is nothing more than the particular daily supports they need anyway to enable them to move around the game board of their life.

For individuals with classic autism who wake up in the morning and must first find their game piece and then get it to the "Go" square on the game board of life, this initial step is much more intensive. I have learned over time how to efficiently streamline the process I refer to as "getting to Go" for students with classic autism. Although it has become the necessary first step to outsmarting explosive behavior for these students (Endow, 2009), it is also a practical way to think about supporting them whether or not they exhibit explosive behavior.

But before we go any further, I want to first address a piece of the equation that is often left out. That is, many times, the best support plans do not work as well as they could because we do not address up-front the needs of those working with our children. So, that is where the next section will take us.

Looking at Ourselves

Safety is one of my initial concerns when beginning a new consultation where extreme behavior is evidenced. Likewise, during the course of working to positively impact behavior, safety remains an ongoing primary concern.

First, student safety is addressed, both in terms of the student exhibiting the behavior and in terms of other students in the room. I will not go into this in detail as it is beyond the scope of this book, except to say that student safety is a number-one concern.

A Positive Beginning to Behavior We Find Challenging

An important part that is often ignored is staff members' perception of their own safety when working with students exhibiting extreme behaviors. Even the youngest and smallest of our students can become stronger than anyone could imagine when they are in the midst of explosive behaviors. When behavior escalates, at a certain point, our students' physiological fight/flight mechanism is triggered. When this happens, the body automatically shifts into survival mode. Nobody in survival mode can use their reasoning abilities. The adrenalin rush bestows upon them indescribable strength and speed.

School personnel in charge of students who regularly get to this point in their explosive behavior can easily become targets of a student "fighting for my life" behavior. It is not unusual for the students' "fighting for my life" behavior to trigger a fear response in the person in charge. If you have ever had the occasion to be that person, you know what I am talking about. It is common for teachers and teaching assistants to become fearful of students who display explosive behavior because of the student's herculean strength when his "fight for my life" survival response kicks in. At this point, there is no backing out of it – the explosion is coming, if not already in progress.

What I have found most important here is to recognize that not all staff members have the same needs. One person may be able to handle the explosive behavior when it happens, but reports "falling apart" afterwards. Another may report that once the escalating behavior gets to a certain point, it is beyond her capacity to be effective with the student as her own fear gets triggered.

Each person working closely with the student must figure out what they need in order to be able to best support the student, both during and after the explosive behavior sequence. Usually, a team approach allows individual team members to do what they are good at and to excuse themselves if the situation is beyond what they have the personal resources to handle.

Though a team approach is optimal, sometimes it is not feasible in a given situation. Indeed, you may never have the luxury of this sort of team approach. That is okay. But then, the adults who find themselves in this situation need to know how they will take care of themselves while remaining responsible for their student when explosive situations arise.

In short, as caregivers, support people, and teachers of those with explosive or extreme behaviors, we need to identify our own needs, plan for them, and meet them if we are going to remain effective and able to stay the course in these sorts of extreme situations. Once having proactively planned for and implemented self-care strategies, most everyone on teams I have worked with have gone on to work successfully and without undue fear. I encourage you to make your plan, follow through, and join our ranks!

One way to think about what your own safety needs might be is to recall past incidents.

   ___   Were you fearful at any point during the incident?

   ___   If so, what might you do differently next time so as to not become fearful?

   ___   Thinking back on the previous incident, do you have safety concerns for yourself?

   ___   If so, what are they, and what actions might you take to better ensure your own safety in the future?

Once you have thought through your safety needs, you will be in a more secure place to start viewing your student's extreme behaviors as possible solutions.

Behavior as Solutions for Students With Classic Autism

For students who have classic autism and extreme behaviors, their behaviors, even the behaviors that hurt themselves or others, often have become solutions to very real problems these students are experiencing. In such situations, I find it helpful to pause and wonder,
- "How's that behavior working for him?" or
- "What problem is that solving for him?"

When I assume that somehow the behavior not only makes sense to the student, but is likely a solution for him, it allows me to validate the student, giving him credit for solving his problem. It also allows me to join with him towards expanding his repertoire of what works – essentially, to offer to him additional solutions that can meet his need while at the same time not injuring him or disrupting the safety or education of others in the environment.

A Positive Beginning to Behavior We Find Challenging

An example would be a student who suddenly drops to the floor in the hallway during passing time and seemingly "won't get up until he's good and ready" to do so. If the student is losing the feel of his body (i.e., sense of proprioception waxing, or not coming in saliently enough to allow him a sense of where his body is located, see page 24), a perfect solution would be to lie down on the floor. The hard surface is helpful in allowing the student to get the feeling of his body back.

In such a situation, a teacher might join with that student, giving him credit for figuring out a solution, and then go on to offer other solutions, such as doing wall push-ups before navigating a busy, crowded hallway (an alternative solution that proactively "beefs up" the proprioception), or give the student a pass that allows him to leave class a few minutes early to avoid the hallway rush of passing time.

Many students with classic autism who have limited or no speaking words do not engage with us as other children do, by, for example, avoiding eye contact, get a bad rap in that people assume they don't care to have relationships with other human beings. We often set about to change their behaviors, especially behaviors that cause physical harm. When doing so, we may forget that these are human beings exhibiting reasonable responses from inside the unpredictable body they were sent to earth in.

When a student is engaging in an unsafe behavior, an immediate response is warranted so no harm will occur. After the immediate crisis, it is often helpful to try to put yourself in your student's shoes, trying to imagine his perception of what was happening given the way his autism dictates his experience.

One way to do this would be to imagine being in the child's situation and then systematically go through all the senses, imagining the particular situation with both a heightened and a diminished experience of each of the senses. In addition, it is wise to take into account that many times our students are dealing with the cumulative effect of several uncomfortable situations across the day.

I have found it makes a world of difference when I assume my student's extreme behavior is somehow reasonable given his experience of the world. Somehow the behavior not only makes sense to him, but also solves a problem he is experiencing. This allows me to join with him towards expanding his solution repertoire.

You may use the very same words and actions whether you are joining with your student – assuming he is responding reasonably given his experience of the world – or whether you are working on a "project" of trying to extinguish his behavior. But somehow the children know whether you are joining with them (requesting relationship) or coming at them (enforcing power and control) trying to fix them. That is, your intent (do you want to establish a relationship or enforce your power?) speaks louder than your words and actions. Be sure to take the opportunity to build a relationship that will set the stage for ongoing positive responses, rather than enforcing a one-time response.

The Difficult Situation

Now that we have a positive framework for looking at our difficult situation, we will go into more detail about the difficult situation. Let's go back to the analogy of the game board put forth in Chapter 1. In the field of autism, we are generally able to support individuals with AS/HFA quite well, but when it comes to individuals with classic autism, the story is a bit different. **Those with classic autism are simply more difficult to support.**

We know that the supports individuals with AS/HFA find valuable are sometimes also helpful to individuals with classic autism, but at other times they seem not to work. It's difficult to explain why sometimes they work and sometimes they don't. Further confounding the situation is that, at times, it seems that we cannot even "reach" some students with classic autism. When that is the case, none of the supports we know and use with individuals with AS/HFA seem to have an impact. Sometimes our sole focus becomes to physically keep students from hurting themselves and others, destroying property, escaping, or some combination thereof.

Individuals with classic autism are different from individuals with AS/HFA. Take the example of hearing too intently. Those with AS/HFA who hear all small sounds know that noise is problematic and generally have supportive measures to resort to, such as wearing ear plugs or headphones, adjusting the volume, etc. Their experience seems to be quite consistent over time. They can pack up a sensory kit containing what they might need (in the case of sensitive hearing, ear plugs, iPod, etc.). This is because their sensory experience, although different from the neurotypical sensory experience, is a generally constant experience that becomes more difficult to cope with when the system is under stress.

When I work with individuals with AS/HFA, I am interested in maintaining their optimal state of regulation. To do so often involves sensory strategies that are both reactive and proactive. The strategy of using ear plugs is *proactive* in that they can be worn before the system is assaulted with loud sound. In addition, the same strategy in the same situation can be a *reactive* strategy in that as soon as the noise begins to be bothersome the ear plugs can be used.

Using the same example of hearing too intently, the way in which individuals with classic autism experience this seems to differ, in that they never know when noises will be perceived by their hearing as too loud or for how long the "too loud" experience will last. In addition, they often don't know which "flavor" of "too loud" they will get.

 I never know if the too loud will be high pitched, have a warped quality or a rushing-wind sort of feel to it, besides the volume being too high. In addition, the loud sound may last for hours inside my body even though the real sound may have lasted only for a few minutes. For example, when an ambulance or fire truck goes by, the sound of the siren has passed after a few moments, but the experience of that sound stays in my body for several hours. To make it even more unpredictable, the whole experience – or maybe only part of the experience – could drop in and out randomly, or it might slowly fade away after a time – maybe a long time or maybe a short time. **One thing that remains constant is that I can never predict or have any way of knowing what will happen when or how long it might last!**

So even though individuals with AS/HFA are similar to individuals with classic autism in that most of their sensory experiences are not the same as neurotypical sensory experiences, unlike their counterparts with AS/HFA, those with classic autism live with a constant unknown in that they cannot predict ahead of time which sensory system might be effected, in what way, and for how long. This translates to an ever-present heightened sense of awareness and anxiety. This constant surprise in fluctuation means a pretty constant level of need to intentionally employ proactive strategies to help our systems maintain a functional level of regulation.

Practical Solutions for Stabilizing Students With Classic Autism to Be Ready to Learn

Although I gave an AS/HFA and a classic autism example above, real life is not as clear-cut. There can be quite an overlap in individual experiences. I have just found it to be an effective way for me to begin thinking of this as I meet and start to sort out the needs of various students.

Internally, the neurology of individuals on the autism spectrum does not seem to automatically regulate their sensory or emotional systems. In addition, they do not tend to automatically pick up necessary cues so as to make sense of the world around them. Often their internal regulation, or lack of regulation, does not allow them to pick up these cues from the world around them, even if they know where to look for them.

In addition, many individuals with classic autism seem to have **neurological movement differences** (Donnellan, Hill, & Leary, 2010; Donnellan, Leary, & Robledo, 2006; Dziuk et al., 2007; Freitag, Kleser, Schneider, & von Gontard, 2007; Leary & Hill, 1996; Maurer & Damasio, 1982; Staples & Reid, 2009). When these movement differences play out in our bodies, it is easy for onlookers to see, as we may get stuck in one position or engage in repetitive movement. Sometimes there can be difficulty in getting a body movement going; at other times, once our body is in motion, we cannot stop even if we want to. Movement differences can also play out in thoughts, speech, and emotions, areas that are not as readily observable to onlookers, yet can be daily obstacles to outsmart for some of us.

Furthermore, external regulation does not seem to be automatically computed by most individuals with classic autism. As a group, we seem to have varying degrees of difficulty in making sense of the information we take in from the world around us. Sometimes we do not know which cues around us are the most salient in which situations. We don't always pick up on when one situation is over and another begins, whether it is a subject in school or a topic of conversation. To many of us, it often feels as if we just don't quite fit into the world.

Neither internal (automatic regulation of sensory system and emotions) nor external (automatic awareness and processing of what is happening in the world around us) regulation just happens for individuals on the autism spectrum. They must bring deliberate and ongoing attention to these areas.

A helpful way to look at this situation is that finding the person's "game piece" is the internal regulation that needs to be in place. Then, once the game piece has been found, it is the external regulation that allows the game piece to be placed on the "Go" square of the game board. It is only after we have gotten to "Go" that we are ready to begin to play the game – to engage with those around us and to live our life, so to speak.

For example, when high school student Chris arrives at school each morning, he spends his first class period swimming laps in the pool. This provides Chris with the internal organization his sensory system needs, effectively allowing him to find his game piece. By the time first period comes to an end, Chris is ready to engage in the day. To do so, he relies on his visual schedule to enable him to track and participate in what is going on in the world around him, providing him with the external regulation that allows him to play his "game of life."

 I think of myself as being either well regulated or not well regulated. When I am well regulated, I am able to fully engage in what is going on around me. My physical movements and my thought processing are fluid. My reaction time to the spoken words of others and to extraneous stimuli is not much different from the reaction time of neurotypicals around me.

But when I am not well regulated, I am less able to engage in what is going on around me. It takes me much longer to process my thoughts, and, thus, my reaction time to the spoken words of others is much slower, and my reactions to extraneous stimuli become bigger and louder and last longer. I am told that my voice becomes louder and that I have a startle response to stimuli that normally would not cause me to startle.

When I am not well regulated, I also have significantly more movement issues. I must bring conscious thought to my physical movement, such as walking, grasping, and chewing. It becomes difficult to engage in multiple movements at the same time, such as walking over to a person and handing him something. First, I have to walk over to the person, stop, and then execute the handing-something motion. It also becomes difficult to combine physical movement with thinking. This means that I have to stop moving in order to think any thoughts unrelated to the actual act of moving my body through space. As a result, it is nearly impossible for me to walk and talk at the same time.

Until science advances enough to enable us to better understand and impact our neurological movement glitches, many of us with classic autism can learn to proactively outsmart at least some of the movement difficulties we experience by addressing our internal and external regulation needs. That is what the remainder, in fact, the centerpiece, of this book is about. Specifically, Chapter 3 will address internal regulation, and Chapter 4 will address external regulation.

Chapter 3
Internal Regulation

Numerous resources have been developed to address the sensory aspects of autism. This book will not repeat what is easily and readily available from other reputable sources (e.g., Brack, 2004, 2009; Dunn, 2008; Kerstein, 2008; Koomar et al., 2007; Kranowitz, 1998; Myles et al., 2000). Something we can very basically and practically synthesize from the numerous sources on this topic available today is that **internal regulation is a high-need area for many with autism spectrum disorders (ASD), most especially those with classic autism.**

In this chapter we will look at the three major components of internal regulation. First of all, **physical concerns** must be addressed because, if a child is not feeling well, is in chronic or acute discomfort, other efforts to assist him in becoming better regulated will not be very effective. The other two major areas discussed to support internal regulation are the **sensory system** and **emotional regulation**.

Physical Well-Being

Before behavior can begin to be assessed, and before sensory needs can begin to be discovered and met, we must resolve any physical problems the child may have. **It is unreasonable to treat behavior that is the result of pain and discomfort as anything but communication of pain and discomfort.** Yet, that is often what happens for students who are not able to tell about their pain. A thorough physical and dental examination should be sought to rule out any underlying physical ailments. This is so basic, and yet very frequently it is not done.

At other times, it is done but with dismal results. Unfortunately, not all physicians have an accurate understanding of autism. If, as a parent or close caregiver, you suspect that your child's behavior is due to him being physically uncomfortable or in pain, you are likely right. Please do not accept the circular sort of reasoning that says your child's behavior is "all the autism" and that we know he has autism because of his behavior. **Behavior does not equal autism. Autism does not equal behavior.**

My advice to parents who believe their child's behavior is at least in part due to pain or physical discomfort is to trust their instincts. They are more than likely correct. Sometimes this means that more than one doctor must be consulted. It is often helpful for parents to find a parent network or support group where they can ask other parents which physicians in town will investigate a child's source of pain rather than dismiss it as "the autism."

The issue of pain and illness is challenging for the following reasons: (a) the student may have difficulty experiencing the location and level/intensity of the pain and discomfort; and (b) the student may not have adequate communication skills to convey his or her sensations and feelings of pain.

There are three main categories of physical illness and well-being to focus on in students with autism: acute physical ailments, chronic physical ailments, and daily physical well-being.

Acute Physical Ailments

These are sicknesses that come on suddenly and are easily remedied, such as an ear infection or pain from an abscessed tooth. Sometimes physical symptoms like a high fever can give a clue, but at other times the pain may be just as intense but no fever is present such as in a hair-line fracture of a bone or torn cartilage. Many times children with classic autism are not able to directly tell you about the pain they feel. So, although it seems that we should be able to easily identify an acute physical ailment, this is not always the case.

Chronic Physical Ailments

Even more difficult to identify just by looking at a child are chronic physical ailments such as the gastrointestinal issues or allergies that are common in many with autism (Kazek et al., 2010; Valicenti-McDermott et al., 2008). Some of these ongoing chronic conditions are very painful and unfortunately go unaddressed for long periods time, sometimes years. Ultimately, such lack of attention can lead to a child's death.

We need to make certain that our children are not suffering from ongoing chronic medical conditions that, if treated, would alleviate or greatly reduce their pain. This may mean seeking second opinions, if parents get the sense that an issue is not taken seriously by a physician, in part because of a lack of understanding of ASD and related conditions. After all, how happy and content would any of us be in our daily lives if every day we had to cope with severe and/ or persistent pain? Would we want someone to try to modify our behavior so we might learn to keep our reactions to a minimum and thus keep our physical pain a better secret? It is unreasonable and unfathomable to put this on our children only because they have autism.

Daily Physical Well-Being

Besides acute and chronic illnesses, we also need to devote attention to children's daily physical well-being. For example, fatigue, hunger, thirst, or inadequate sleep makes all of us irritable and more difficult to deal with. Why would it be any different for children just because they have autism? In fact, most individuals with autism have additional physical discomforts due to an extra sensitive sensory system. It is not at all unusual for everyday sights, sounds, smells, tastes, and things touching their skin to cause them to feel physical discomfort, sometimes even pain. They may not be able to tell you, but watch closely because they will likely give you clues. Clues can include (a) body postures and movements, especially if new to the child; (b) a more severe or quicker-than-usual move toward shutdown state or meltdown; and (c) a seeming unwillingness to engage in previously enjoyed activities. **Any new unusual behaviors should automatically raise a flag as potentially masking an underlying physical difficulty.** When any obstacles in these three areas are removed, we are in a much better place to move ahead with assessing a child's internal regulation needs.

Sensory Regulation

We will now look at differences in taking in and processing sensory information, along with how to support sensory regulation by using a sensory profile addressing the practical concerns that arise in a school setting when a sensory diet is implemented (*sensory profile* is the author's choice of words to refer to sensory needs; it does not refer to assessment tools incorporating the term in their titles).

Taking in Sensory Information

All of us take in information from the world around us through our senses. We have the five senses we all learn in grade school – visual (sight), olfactory (smell), gustatory (taste), auditory (hearing), and tactile (touch). We also have a sense called proprioception (body awareness) and another called vestibular (balance). The chart on page 24 lists our seven sensory systems along with their locations and functions.

Location and Functions of the Sensory Systems

System	Location	Function
Tactile (touch)	**Skin** – density of cell distribution varies throughout the body. Areas of greatest density include mouth, hands, and genitals.	Provides information about the environment and object qualities (touch, pressure, texture, hard, soft, sharp, dull, heat, cold, pain).
Vestibular (balance)	**Inner ear** – stimulated by head movements and input from other senses, especially visual.	Provides information about where our body is in space, and whether or not we or our surroundings are moving. Tells about speed and direction of movement.
Proprioception (body awareness)	**Muscles and joints** – activated by muscle contractions and movement.	Provides information about where a certain body part is and how it is moving.
Visual (sight)	**Retina of the eye** – stimulated by light.	Provides information about objects and persons. Helps us define boundaries as we move through time and space.
Auditory (hearing)	**Inner ear** – stimulated by air/sound waves.	Provides information about sounds in the environment (loud, soft, high, low, near, far).
Gustatory (taste)	**Chemical receptors in the tongue** – closely entwined with the olfactory (smell) system.	Provides information about different types of taste (sweet, sour, bitter, salty, spicy).
Olfactory (smell)	**Chemical receptors in the nasal structure** – closely associated with the gustatory system.	Provides information about different types of smell (musty, acrid, putrid, flowery, pungent).

From Myles, B. S., Cook, K. T., Miller, N. E., Rinner, L., & Robbins, L. A. (2000). *Asperger syndrome and sensory issues: Practical solutions for making sense of the world.* Shawnee Mission, KS: Autism Asperger Publishing Company; p. 5. Reprinted with permission.

Internal Regulation

These seven senses work together to bring us information from the world around us. For people with ASD, the information gained from the senses sometimes comes a bit differently than it seems to come to people without autism. The three main effects of this difference is that information may come in **too big, too small,** or **distorted**. This can happen in any, some, or all of the senses. For example, a particular sense that is too big in the morning may be too small in the afternoon. Further, one sense may be okay, one sense may be too big, and a third may be distorted all at the same time.

When this happens, the world can feel unsafe or dangerous. It can feel like being in one of those mirror-distortion houses at carnivals. Imagine if that experience was thrust upon you and you didn't know what was what – which experiences were real and which were illusions – and furthermore, that you had no way of knowing when it would stop. This can precipitate varying reactions, from the feeling that one has physically disappeared or, the opposite, has become too large to fit through doorway, to the movement sensation that being on a small boat in turbulent water can bring even if, in reality, your body is standing completely still on solid ground.

Sensory regulation involves actively adjusting amounts and kinds of incoming sensory information in a way that allows for optimal functioning because one's neurology does not permit this to occur automatically.

To complicate matters, similar experiences often elicit a multitude of physiological responses, and a person with classic autism never knows ahead of time how his nervous system will interpret incoming information or how his brain will process it. This means that the person constantly needs to be "on guard" in terms of watching his behavioral responses – the more disregulated they become, the more of a challenge it is to deal with even the most ordinary events of the day.

 As an autistic person, how comfortable I am able to live my everyday life depends on how well regulated I have taken the time to become on a given day. When I am not well regulated, I can count on having difficulties with managing my behavior. When it comes to sensory regulation, it's just plain smart to stay on top of it!

Processing Sensory Information

Besides differences in the way sensory information comes to individuals with autism, once there, the information may be processed differently, too. Although there are several ways people on the spectrum process information, three ways seem to impact them most: linear, mono channel, and nondiscriminatory processing (Attwood, 2007).

Linear processing happens when information is processed using one sense at a time. So, first the child may process a loud shrill sound that is unattached to anything because he processes sound first. Then, in moments, or maybe in minutes, he processes what he sees. Next he might process the movement. Thus, even though he was standing on the playground when a police car with sirens and flashing lights went by, he may not connect the sound of the siren to the police car, simply because it was not processed as a whole. Instead, it was processed in a linear fashion – first the sound of the siren, then the sight of the flashing lights on the police car, then the movement of the police car as it traveled down the street. If the process is interrupted midstream, the learner may have to begin the processing at the beginning (first step).

It takes longer to process information one sense at a time than when individual senses are processed simultaneously as a whole experience. Thus, when receiving a handout in class, for example, a student with autism might first have to process the feel of the paper in his hand, moving the paper to his desk, popping up the picture of the pencil in his mind, going through the motions of actually getting out a pencil, and only then, might he be able to attend to what's next – completing the worksheet. And if the verbal instructions have already been given, the student has missed them because his linear processing meant that he first processed feel, then sight, and then sound. If the sound – the teacher's verbal directions – happened before the student's processing lineup (one sense at a time) was up to sound, he very likely has missed it.

Sample of sensory characteristics of the typical child with AS/HFA.

From Myles, B. S., Cook, K. T., Miller, N. E., Rinner, L., & Robbins, L. A. (2000). *Asperger Syndrome and sensory issues: Practical solutions for making sense of the world.* Shawnee Mission, KS: Autism Asperger Publishing Company. Used with permission.

Internal Regulation

Most often when this happens, students are told to pay attention or to focus. The truth is, they were paying attention and were focusing on the information deemed relevant in the moment by their linear sensory processing.

Mono-channel processing refers to using a preferred sense to process all information. It is not that a student makes a conscious choice and prefers one sense over another; rather, his neurology seems to dictate this by making information available to him in this way. Thus, a student may not be able to process the words you are saying if he has been told to look at you (eye contact) while you are saying them. He may only have one channel available with which to process incoming information. This forces a choice. If the teacher indicates she wants a student to listen to the important information she will be saying, some of our students with autism will automatically look away from the teacher.

If the student can only process using one channel, it makes sense that if it is important to hear what the teacher is saying, the student will not look at the teacher so that he indeed might hear! So outward appearances to the contrary, see how compliant it is for this student to quickly turn away from the center of instruction when his teacher says, "Pay attention to what I am saying!"

Nondiscriminatory processing refers to all incoming information getting processed equally. Individuals with autism do not consciously have any choice about this. Nor do they decide how to process information in any given situation. It just happens!

For example, when a student processes incoming information in a nondiscriminatory style, this may mean that while he is in the library, the hum of computers, the sparkles seen from fluorescent lights, the reflection of the light on the table top, the movement of other students, the various smells of old, dried paper and book bindings, along with feeling too warm and having one shoelace tied more tightly than the other, all attract his attention just as saliently as the purpose for which he is in the library – to find and check out a book.

With each bit of information coming in equally salient, it is difficult to know where to focus one's attention. It is truly amazing that anything at all gets accomplished when a student has a nondiscriminatory style of processing!

For me, all information tends to come in pretty equally, which poses its own set of problems. For example, when I am speaking at a conference, the luminescent particles I can see in the air cascading down from the fluorescent lights and the sound of the building's ventilation system cycling come in just as saliently as the information I am to present on to the audience. I cognitively understand background noise but have never experienced any noise as "in the background." For me, all information tends to come in equally – I most often have a nondiscriminatory processing style. When driving a car, I must use my cognition to remind myself that the road signs are more important information to pay attention to than the leaves on the trees because both visual stimuli come in equally.

Sensory regulation allows us specific times and the necessary supports to adjust the impact of the amounts and kinds of incoming information so that we can process that information most effectively, which in turn allows us to function optimally in the world around us. We need sensory breaks during which to accomplish this because our neurology does not allow it to happen automatically. More in-depth discussion and strategies concerning sensory breaks are provided in a later section of this book (see pages 40-56).

Common Patterns of Sensory Processing

Dunn (2008, pp. 146-147) outlines four patterns of sensory processing in individuals with autism spectrum disorders and defines them in the following way.

1. **Seeking**

   Children who fall into this category add movement, touch, sound, and visual stimuli to every life event. Seekers make noise, fidget in their seats, touch everything, feel objects, touch and hang on to others, or chew on things. Each of these actions intensifies the sensory input, which, in turn, increases the child's chances of meeting high thresholds. Children in this category may lack caution in play, display excitability, and engage in impulsive behavior in an attempt to increase sensory input (Dunn, 1997).

2. **Low Registration**

   Children in this group do not notice what is going on around them, so they may seem dull, uninterested, or oblivious to what goes on around them (Dunn, 1997). Further, they may seem withdrawn, difficult to engage, or self-absorbed; they may also be easily exhausted and appear apathetic (National Center for Clinical Infant Programs/

Zero to Three [NCCIP], 1994). The brain is not activating enough to cue the child about what is going on. Highly salient sensory input is needed to get these children's attention so they can participate in school activities.

3. **Sensitivity**

Children in this group have low thresholds and passive self-regulation. They tend to be hyperactive, distracted, and easily upset because they notice more things than their peers (Dunn, 1997). Not surprisingly, children with sensitivity have difficulty completing tasks, as new stimuli capture their attention repeatedly during the day. They may also have difficulty learning from their experiences because routines are disrupted so often that they cannot complete tasks and learn (NCCIP, 1994).

4. **Avoiding**

Children in this group actively work to reduce input. They are resistant and unwilling to participate, particularly in unfamiliar activities. They experience discomfort quickly, and to keep from feeling discomfort, they reduce their activity and withdraw.

Using a Sensory Profile to Support Regulation

Sensory regulation is maintained by employing a mix of proactive and reactive (see pages 40-41) sensory strategies throughout the day so the student can maintain an alertness level optimal for learning.

This is accomplished through the use of a "sensory diet" that is prescribed by an occupational therapist (OT) to specifically meet the needs of a particular student's nervous system (Kranowitz, 1998). The associated use of the term "menu" here refers to a list of strategies that have been found useful for a particular student to maintain his sensory regulation.

Think of a sensory diet prescribed by an OT as you would medication prescribed by a physician. Just as we would not put out a tray of medicines and invite our students to help themselves if they feel a need for medication during the school day, we should not have items used for sensory regulation available and then instruct students to help themselves if they feel the need! A sensory diet is best prescribed by an OT based on individual student assessment. **Sensory strategies that support regulation in one student will not necessarily support regulation in another student.**

The goal of using a sensory profile is to allow the student to become better regulated, which in turn supports improved participation during the school day. When students are not well regulated, it interferes with their ability to learn. Students may stop working to seek out sensory input, miss directions and cues because information is not coming in saliently enough, become distracted by the enormous amount of sensory input they take in, or withdraw from learning to reduce sensory input (Dunn, 2008).

Sensory Profile Strategies

Following are examples of ideas you can use with your student/child. The examples and ensuing discussion are sorted out by sensory system. While this makes it easy to read, please remember: **Our sensory systems are not always this neat and tidy. There is seldom only one thing going on at a time!**

 This brief discussion is not intended to take the place of the extensive volumes written about sensory systems and interventions or to be a substitute for a sensory evaluation by a qualified OT. It is merely a starting place to list some common information and practical things to try.

Proprioception

Our proprioceptive sense receives feedback from our joints and muscles as our muscles contract and move. Proprioception is the sense that allows us to feel our body's whereabouts and automatically allows it to coordinate movement without bringing conscious thought to it. For example, we normally know we are sitting on a chair because our joints and muscles give us that feedback. In fact, for those whose proprioception is in good working order, conscious thought does not need to be brought to the task of sitting on a chair.

When my sense of proprioception starts fading, I have to consciously monitor sitting in a chair so that my body doesn't fall out if I move too suddenly or lean a bit too far one way or the other. This is because my joints and muscles don't give me reliable feedback of my body sitting in the chair.

The tricky thing is that there is no alarm system to warn me when my proprioception is starting to fade. Thus, if I do not want to be surprised and do not want to surprise others by falling out of my chair, I must bring conscious attention to the task of monitoring this each day. Some days I'm better at this than others.

Proprioception Solutions

Proprioception involves the push/pull of "heavy work." The need for resistance is most often high. When working with an individual experiencing challenges with proprioception, here are examples of things you might have the student try:

1. Carrying, pushing, or pulling heavy things

2. Intense climbing (stairs, rock walls, stair stepper, elliptical work-out machine, etc.)

3. Vigorous jumping (trampoline, jumping jacks, jumping rope, etc.)

4. Vigorous Wii game playing (also other video games involving vigorous movement such as Dance Dance Revolution)

5. Stationary bike pedaling with high resistance

6. Scooter board

7. Tricycle pedaling with high resistance

8. Moving through water in a swimming pool

9. Vacuuming or vigorous cleaning

10. Intense workout

The impact of proprioceptive input lasts for up to 2 hours (Brack, 2009), so it is easy to see that a once-a-week or even a daily OT consult where the OT is the only person providing a student with access to proprioceptive input is inadequate for meeting the needs of many students. It is great to find naturally occurring opportunities to get the needed input, such as having the student carry a crate of milk cartons to pass out or returning stacks of books to the library. Wearing a heavy backpack while walking between classes is helpful for some students.

Vestibular

The vestibular sense receives feedback from the inner ear and is stimulated by head movements along with input from other senses, especially the visual sense.

It is the vestibular sense that gives us feedback about our body when it is in motion. This feedback translates into a generalized coordination and balance as we move about in the world around us. When the vestibular sense is not giving reliable feedback, all sorts of strange experiences become ours to cope with.

 For me, this often includes having dizzy and/or nauseous feelings. Uncoordinated movements reign, whether I like it or not. In fact, most times I don't anticipate which movements are less fluid than necessary as, once again, the experience is not always consistent over time. Sometimes my movements overshoot my intent – like the time my friend Lisa nearly got a salad with all the fixings dumped into her lap because my body "overshot" when my intent was merely to pass the salad.

Vestibular Solutions

Some students need intense vestibular input. Such a need may be met by any movement involving rotation or spinning. When working with a student experiencing vestibular challenges, here are examples of things you might try:

1. Swings that allow for spinning

2. Sit-and-spin toys (popular among younger students)

3. Allowing the student to spin objects (some find it calming to simply look at spinning gadgets or items)

 Because rotary or spinning activities can be dangerous to the child, these activities should never be done TO the child and should be used only in consult with an experienced occupational therapist.

A less intense sort of input may be obtained from back-and-forth or up-and-down linear movement, such as

1. Rocking in a rocking chair

2. Using a glider chair

3. Jumping rope

4. Climbing stairs or using a stair stepper

5. Doing wall push-ups or chair push-ups

 Often proprioceptive and vestibular needs overlap and it is not practically necessary to sort this out.

Tactile

The tactile sense has to do with touch and the pressure from touch. Many students are sensitive to the feeling of clothing or tags from clothing against their skin, including seams in socks. Some report they experience pain from these kinds of feelings and are not able to tolerate wearing certain types of shoes or clothing. Others seek out the pressure clothing can give and prefer wearing lycra or spandex clothing under regular clothes.

Tactile Solutions

When working with a student experiencing tactile challenges, here are examples of things you might try in collaboration with an OT.

1. Weighted blankets/vests

    Many who seek pressure find weighted blankets to be helpful. A rule of thumb for weighted blankets is that the blanket should not weigh more than 10% of the person's body weight and that the student should be able to remove it independently. Indeed, 5% of the child's body weight is shown by research (VandenBerg, 2001) to be the ideal therapeutic weight.

Weighted vests are an alternative to weighted blanket that are sometimes more practical. OTs commonly recommend that weighted vests be worn for 20 minutes and then be taken off for 1-½ to 2 hours. Research (Fertel-Daley, Bedell, & Hinojosa, 2001) shows positive effects of increased attention, decreasing distractions, and decreasing self-stimulatory behaviors in students wearing weighted vests for up to 2 hours. This simply means that the neurological benefit derived from wearing the weighted vest is likely obtained in 20 minutes, and in some students wearing the vest for more than 2 hours may increase the positive effects. Whenever possible, it is most practical to have the student put on and take off of the vest to coincide with natural transitions in the schedule to avoid extra disruptions for the student.

2. Any texture that produces an organizing effect, such as textured jewelry, fidgets, and vibrating toys or pens

3. Shaving cream, hair gel, or lotions

4. Encouraging the child to touch various textures by having to find a small toy hidden in dry beans and/or rice

For example, a particular sense that is too big in the morning may be too small in the afternoon. Further, one sense may be okay, one sense may be too big, and a third may be distorted at the same time.

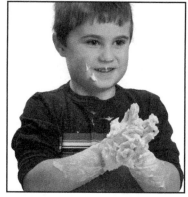

Some students find it helpful to maintain sensory regulation when sensory activities are part of the classroom instruction. An example is finger writing spelling words in shaving cream or in a bin of rice or beans.

Internal Regulation

Pairing sensory modalities with instruction can assist some students in maintaining sensory regulation, but is not sufficient to replace all sensory breaks (see pages 40-56). While it is easy to incorporate sensory-seeking activities into instruction, sensory breaks to cut down on or guard against too much stimulation must be afforded each student so as to keep his sensory system in that "just right" place for learning.

 Sensory needs change over time. For example, when I was a little girl, light touch was very disorganizing to me and actually produced a startle reaction. My body craved deep pressure.

As an adult, I still need deep pressure, and I sleep with a weighted blanket. In addition, my body now experiences certain light touch as organizing, such as light scratching of my hands and forearms by a person wearing textured gloves.

Auditory

Just as for the other senses, some people on the autism spectrum need to cut down the incoming auditory stimulation whereas others need controlled auditory input to stay regulated.

Auditory Solutions

When working with a student experiencing auditory challenges, here are examples of things you might try.

For those needing lowering of auditory input to stay organized:

1. Ear plugs (a practical way to test this out is to purchase a variety of styles of ear plugs from the power tool section of a home improvement store)

2. Headphones (may dampen sounds enough to afford comfort while still allowing the person to hear regular conversation)

For those needing the steady input of auditory stimulation to stay organized:

1. Listening to tabletop water and rock fountain (or other predicable regulated sound)

2. Listening to particular music or perhaps nature sounds via headphones

Visual

Some individuals with autism have a strong need for visually congruent matches in their environment. As a result, it may be important for them to visually organize a room or work space, or perhaps to wear matching clothing or have certain color schemes in projects. Some need the world to "look right" – to somehow appear visually congruent – in order to stay regulated.

 I feel physically dizzy when I walk into a chaotic-looking room. If I stay for long, I become physically sick to my stomach.

When I was younger, people often attributed to me a need to be controlling, but the truth was that if I didn't arrange the environment in a certain way, I would become too dizzy to walk or too physically sick to participate in activities around me. My intent wasn't to be disruptive, but to arrange my surroundings in such a way that I could participate and do what was asked of me.

It is clearly not possible at all times to arrange the world around us according to our needs. Therefore, we often need sensory breaks (see pages 40-56) that allow us to close our eyes or to be in a space with no lights for a time so we can adjust from the constant visual input from the world around us.

Visual Solutions

When working with a student experiencing visual challenges, here are examples of things you might have your student try.

1. Taking breaks in a visually neutral or quiet environment

2. Looking at a filtered fish tank

3. Watching a soothing screen saver

4. Watching water-and-oil toys where the oil droplets filter slowly through the water

5. Engaging in soothing one-player online or handheld games with repeating color patterns such as Bejeweled, Pop Groups, Bubble Blaster (some find these sorts of games to produce a more "revved-up" rather than calming effect, so evaluate for each individual)

Sometimes brightness is a factor, especially in schools where fluorescent lighting can produce a shining glare off white paper. If you suspect this might be a problem for a student, try these alternatives:

1. Printing work sheets on pastel-colored paper instead of white

2. Using pastel-colored transparencies over print on a white background

3. Using laptop versus desktop computers. Computer screen brightness can be a huge problem. Many prefer laptops as the lighting behind the screen is tolerable to them, whereas the lighting behind the screen in a desktop computer is unworkable. However, some don't even realize there is a difference! So, again, it is a matter of meeting the needs of the individual.

4. Using natural lighting or incandescent light bulbs when possible, as fluorescent lights can be problematic.

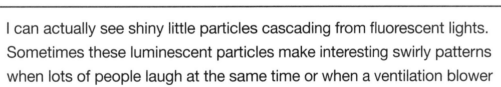

I can actually see shiny little particles cascading from fluorescent lights. Sometimes these luminescent particles make interesting swirly patterns when lots of people laugh at the same time or when a ventilation blower kicks in. As a child, I got reprimanded for laughing inappropriately when this happened, but it did look very amusing to me.

5. Using colored lenses. Some have reported benefit from wearing colored lenses. A practical way to determine if this might make a difference for you or for your student would be to try on several inexpensive colored sunglasses to see if a certain color seems to be helpful.

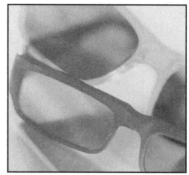

Taste (Oral/Motor)

The sense of taste encompasses more than just how food tastes. It also includes the chewing and sucking involved in the eating process along with the feel of the texture and temperature of the food in our mouths. Many individuals with classic autism have difficulties with some aspect of taste and eating.

Taste Solutions

When working with a student experiencing challenges with taste, here are examples of things you might try.

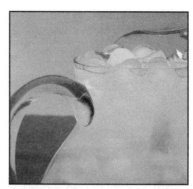

1. Many have a spicy and sour taste preference, and this may be utilized to adjust alertness level if eating or drinking fits into the overall classroom.
   - sour candy warheads
   - vinegar chips
   - lemon juice in drinks
   - pickles
   - jalapenos, or jalapeno-flavored foods (I knew of one student who often ate jalapenos as his preferred and only pizza topping!)

2. Some students find resistive sucking through a straw to be organizing, this may include ...
   - thick shakes
   - applesauce
   - pudding

3. If intense crunch or lots of chewing is organizing to the
    student, try offering …
    –   raw veggies
    –   hard apples
    –   tough-to-chew licorice or gummy bears
    –   bagels or bagel chips
    –   Bavarian pretzels
    –   chewing gum
    –   twice-toasted bread or large crunchy croutons

 If an individual has significant oral/motor needs, there is a propensity for
excess weight gain. It is far easier to adjust food intake to prevent undue
weight gain than to try to lose the weight after it has been gained.

Smell (Olfactory)

Some of us perceive smell to such an uncomfortable degree that we need to employ
strategies to mask or block odors that are too overwhelming for us.

Smell Solutions

When working with an individual experiencing challenges with smell here are examples of
things you might try.

1. Closing the door to the kitchen when cooking

2. Having the student hold something, such as a scented
    cloth or tissue lightly over his nose

3. Helping build tolerance over time (if there is an especially
    difficult odor that is also an odor common to the every-
    day environment, it may be helpful to try building up a
    tolerance to it so as to not be limited by the offending
    odor)

4. Allowing a break from all the environmental sensory input; this often helps to reset the
   system to be ready to cope again

5. Masking environmental odors by using …
   - scented candles
   - heated scented oils
   - diffusers
   - room fresheners
   - linen sprays
   - scented tissues

 I used to wear a necklace that was a miniature cork-topped bottle with decorative foliage inside to which a few drops of mint were added. When an obnoxious odor would find me, I took a few sniffs of the mint to cope.

Implementing Sensory Breaks

If most days your student has periods of appearing **hyper or anxious,** has periods of exhibiting **low tone** (when her muscle tone appears "loose and floppy"), or zoning out, or both, automatically insert **proactive sensory breaks.** This means that sensory breaks are placed directly into the student's schedule, as opposed to being added when signs of disregulation appear.

The purpose of a sensory break is to keep the student's sensory system regulated so he will be in a position to learn. Although the term *sensory break* is widely used in the field of autism, I think we have done our students a disservice by using that particular term. The term *break* first of all implies that we've earned it by working hard. Also, the general idea of a break is that it's a time to kick back, relax, and have fun. For an autistic, a sensory break is none of this. It is hard work to manually regulate our sensory system.

Most students with classic autism and some with Asperger Syndrome/HFA need regularly scheduled breaks to maintain sensory regulation just like your diabetic student needs insulin to maintain metabolic regulation. The idea is to provide enough proactive sensory breaks to generally keep the student in that "just right" place (Case-Smith & Arbesman, 2008; Williams & Shellenberger, 1996) for learning. In addition, some students need sensory input during a given activity. Examples include sitting on a wiggle seat, having a fidget, and spelling words in shaving cream.

Think of the sensory break as needed medications and the sensory profile as the type and dosage of the particular medications. As such, you will need a qualified OT to prescribe the protocol just as a diabetic student needs a physician to prescribe his medication. The reason we bring regulation to students, whether it is metabolic regulation for the diabetic or sensory regulation for the student with autism, is to enable students to learn efficiently and effectively.

 For students with classic autism, regulation is often a basic necessity in that, if they are not regulated, they will not be in a place to learn, no matter how good the teaching might be!

Some days pose more stress to the sensory system than others. These are the days when you will add **reactive sensory breaks** to the already scheduled proactive breaks. Practically speaking, this means that before the time of the next proactive sensory break, your student will begin to show signs of needing it (react to the situation). Examples of common ways in which students show they need an extra break include being less able to concentrate, move, or speak fluidly; showing a change in voice volume; more intense body movement; and a sudden change in mood, such as becoming irritable or silly.

As soon as this happens, show the student it is break time and help her to take her break. It is a good idea to use a visual break card to show when a break will happen.

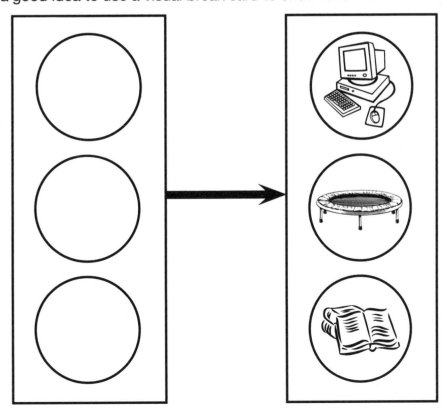

The break card shown on page 41 allows three sensory choices to be included – one in each circle. Some students need the break card inserted into their schedules to show them that an extra break will happen just now (see page 69).

How Long Should Sensory Breaks Be?
(After All, This Is School and I Don't Want My Student Missing out on Classroom Instruction ...)

No exact length of time can be specified for a sensory break. Remember, the purpose of a sensory break is to keep the sensory system regulated so the student can be in a position to learn. Sometimes this takes a few minutes, and at other times it can take most of the day.

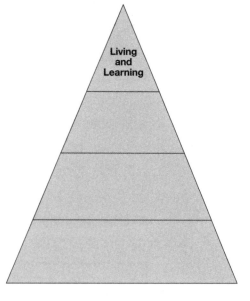

Allowing sensory breaks is often difficult for teachers because their mission is to teach. They become concerned when their students miss out on classroom learning opportunities due to their sensory breaks. This is a valid concern that comes from good teachers who want to teach their students.

Here is the explanation I give: Most students come to school ready to learn. In the triangle chart at the right, living and learning are at the top.

Assuming any underlying physical needs have been addressed (see pages 21-23), regulation is the foundation. Regulation is the path by which students will get an opportunity for their bodies to be in a place where they can learn.

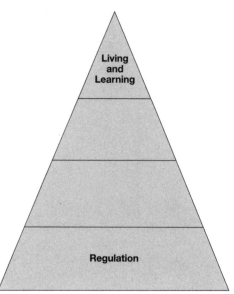

This book concerns the regulation piece of this triangle model. But let's take a brief look at the rest of the model to see how it ties into good teaching and supports the construction of individualized education program (IEP) goals.

Internal Regulation

You can use this triangle model to help ensure your student's IEP includes goals in each of these main areas – regulation, relationship (social development), communication, and academic/preacademic learning/ life skills.

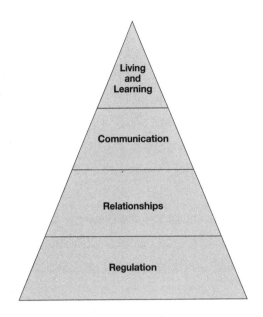

Once you have developed goals for all four areas of the triangle, teaching becomes easier, because you have just given yourself permission to do a good job, working on your student's IEP goals, no matter which layer of the triangle the student's needs take you to at any given moment!

So, if you are teaching and things start to not go so well, set aside your academic teaching goals for the moment and drop to the base of the triangle. Now you will engage your student in regulation. Whenever something isn't working well for your student, go to the base of the triangle and work there. **Everything else is dependent on your student being well regulated.** Once the students' regulation needs are met, you move up, using your relationship with the student and communication to get him back into the learning environment, with each step of the triangle providing opportunities to work toward IEP goals.

If you use this simple model, it will not matter how long regulation takes, because you will be doing exactly what you are supposed to be doing – working on the regulation goals in your student's IEP. This is not wasted time away from instruction. It is a necessary lifelong skill for everyone – including any person with classic autism – to learn how to keep oneself well regulated in a body headed up by a neurology that does not automatically do this on its own.

Sample IEP goals:

External Regulation or Internal Sensory Regulation – proactive Sensory Breaks (listed in order of complexity)

- Aaron will be in the presence of the adult putting together his daily visual schedule while the adult points out the (proactive) sensory regulation breaks in the schedule.

- Aaron will assist in constructing his daily visual schedule by placing the (proactive) sensory regulation breaks into the schedule.

- Aaron will construct his daily visual schedule by matching a preprinted picture of his daily visual schedule that includes (proactive) sensory regulation breaks (break into steps, inserting how much of his schedule he will construct or with what kind of support he will need to do this, gradually leading to independence).

Note: Add criteria for measurement, for example: 80% of weekly opportunities for eight consecutive weeks.

Location of Sensory Breaks

Because OTs generally see students who have high sensory needs, we can get into the rut of sending our students to the OT room for all their sensory breaks.

I view OTs as resource people who help to develop sensory break plans, not just the folks who administer the breaks. Think of all the locations where students might take a sensory break: at their desk, at the back of the classroom, in the resource room, in the hallway outside the classroom, in the various locations in the building, in the OT room, and outdoors.

Here is a short list of examples to stimulate your thinking in terms of utilizing areas where students have gone to regulate themselves, along with the regulation activities they engaged in at the various locations.

At the desk:
- Feeling different textures glued to the underside of the desk (*tactile*)
- Manipulating a fidget (*tactile, visual, proprioceptive*)
- Wearing ear plugs or sound-blocking headphones (*auditory*)
- Chewing gum (*oral/motor*)
- Using a wiggle cushion, weighted vest, or weighted lap blanket (*proprioceptive*)
- Chair push-ups (*proprioceptive*)

In the back of the classroom:
- Using beanbag chair (*proprioceptive, tactile*)
- Using a small pop-up tent to screen out/lower the effects on visual and oral stimuli (*auditory, visual*)
- Using swing or rocking chair (*proprioceptive, vestibular*)
- Walking or pacing – some teachers put a strip of masking tape on the floor to mark where the student can pace (*proprioceptive*)

In the hallway outside the classroom:
- Wall push-ups (*proprioceptive*)
- Jumping on a small floor trampoline (*proprioceptive, vestibular*)
- Taking a walk (*proprioceptive, auditory, visual*)
- Using a pogo stick, scooter board, tricycle with resistance (*proprioceptive, vestibular*)

The Changing Frequency and Duration of Sensory Breaks

One more thing to be aware of: **The frequency and duration of sensory breaks can change over time.** Just because a 10-minute break three times a day or a 30-minute break upon arrival at school works now, it doesn't mean it will work well forever. So many variables are involved that we can pretty much count on the fact that as our students grow and change and master new skills in forever-changing environments, the sensory needs of their forever-developing and changing bodies will change, too. Thus, our efforts to support them must adjust to the demands of their sensory system.

If your student becomes less regulated over time by, as evidenced, for example, by making extraneous noises, increased fidgeting or distractibility, marked decrease in movement, or attempts at blocking sensory input such as covering ears, squinting, or closing eyes, it is a clue that his sensory needs may have changed. When this happens, the most expedient way to get it sorted out is to request a re-evaluation or a consultation by an OT if that option is available to you. In addition, you will likely benefit from reading some books on the subject. Several are listed in the reference section at the end of this book. The more you learn about the subject, the better you will be able to help and support your students.

Sensory Profiles and Meltdowns

As emphasized throughout, **it is important to use sensory strategies proactively every day to maintain regulation**, which prevents meltdowns. Use of sensory strategies during meltdowns, especially sensory input strategies (like trying to get the student to put on a weighted vest to provide deep pressure or offering crunchy food or an iPod with music), often triggers or intensifies the biological fight/flight response (see page 13).

An example is the student who runs out of the room when you try to get him into his rocking chair – the same chair that otherwise has a calming affect on him. He runs because at the time he is experiencing a biological fight/flight response, which means that the introduction of any kind of input is perceived as a threat to his life, thus intensifying the fight-or-flight survival reaction. This, in turn, can serve to heighten meltdown behavior. Therefore, **do not try to use sensory input strategies during the height of a meltdown.**

Children with classic autism will likely not outgrow their sensory needs, but their sensory needs will change over time. The goal is, as they grow up, to teach them how to recognize their needs and then request and implement optimal sensory regulation as independently as possible.

Managing Sensory Differences in Inclusive Settings

Students with classic autism need sensory regulation opportunities every day just as if it was medicine; no questions asked. We know they have autism, and the regulation of their sensory system needs to be supported proactively – on a regular basis ahead of any problem or presenting need – with both **sensory guarding** and **sensory input** for them to function well. Sensory guarding is the act of actively preventing sensory input. A few examples of how sensory guarding is seen in behavior include putting hands over ears to block sound or sitting still as a statue to avoid clothing tags from moving against the skin.

When students with autism need input to support their sensory regulation, such as a wiggle cushion, fidgets, chewy or crunchy foods, sunglasses, etc., these items must be looked at as if they are prescription medicine. They are necessary to maintain sensory regulation just as insulin is necessary to a diabetic to maintain metabolic regulation.

We would never think of sharing our diabetic student's insulin with all the other students because we might be concerned that it isn't fair that diabetics get insulin and the rest of the students don't (LaVoie, 1994). Yet, I have seen well-meaning teachers use this sort of reasoning when it comes to sensory items, insisting students with ASD share their "medicine" with all the other students because that is what is "fair."

This isn't an easy concept to grasp. After all, it is tempting to look at a fidget as a toy rather than seeing it on par with medication, which it can be for students with autism. So, if we see the fidget as a toy and the OT's swing as play equipment, it would be reasonable that we would try to teach the age-old concept of sharing toys with classmates. This is why it is so important to understand sensory regulation and to understand how a particular student stays regulated.

It is also important to explain this to classmates. To do so, choose from a variety of storybooks written for different age levels of students that can be read to classmates, videos that can be watched, and group exercises that allow students to have a sensory experience similar to what their classmate with classic autism may experience. (See suggestions under Recommended Resources.)

In a classroom situation, it is a good idea to allow students to try out or have a turn with any special equipment used by the student with autism that may look like a toy or indoor playground equipment, so as to quell curiosity. This should be followed by some common-sense classroom guideline such as, "Any student may ask to use the rocking chair when it is not in use, but because Sam needs the rocking chair, he will be able to use it every day whenever his body needs it."

I have never run into students who do not understand this distinction. In fact, once it has been explained to students why Sam needs to use the rocking chair, they are typically very willing to accommodate the need.

What is fair in a school setting is that each student gets what he or she needs in order to learn. For one student that may be insulin, for another it might be verbal praise, and for a student with autism it might be wearing sunglasses or a visor to lessen the sensory discomfort imposed by fluorescent lights. **Proactive sensory breaks for students with classic autism need to be put in place right on their daily schedule just as insulin injections are for students with diabetes.**

It is not unusual for a person with diabetes to need to adjust the amount and/or frequency of insulin he needs when his body is under stress, such as if he is experiencing a physical ailment or emotional upheaval. The same can happen with students with autism. So, besides having the regularly scheduled proactive sensory breaks in place, students with autism need additional reactive sensory breaks in response to their experiences of stress. **Thus, an individualized combination of proactive and reactive sensory breaks will likely best meet the needs of students with classic autism.**

 Remember sensory breaks can occur without leaving the environment.

Just as we don't expect diabetic students to prescribe their own insulin, we should not expect students with ASD to prescribe their own sensory diet. This is a prescriptive measure based on assessment by an OT well versed in sensory interventions.

 We need to clearly distinguish necessary supports from reward systems. Both have their time and place for our students, but just as diabetics are never expected to earn their insulin, individuals with autism should never be expected to earn their supports, sensory breaks included!

Figuring out Sensory Profile and Regulation Strategies

Val Paradiz has developed an excellent resource to help those of us on the autism spectrum to figure out our sensory diet needs and regulation strategies. Her focus on doing so is to ultimately allow the person with ASD to be in a position to effectively self-advocate. Val's unit on The Sensory Scan from *The Integrated Self-Advocacy ISA® Curriculum: A Program for Emerging Self-Advocates with Autism Spectrum and Other Conditions* – Student Workbook (2009) – appears here as a very practical resource for us as we go about the business of supporting our students with classic autism.

Students with classic autism can learn to become effective self-advocates. The first step in the process for all self-advocates, including students with classic autism, is to become aware of their own needs. The Sensory Profile is presented as a paper/pencil inventory for the student to fill out. If you are supporting a student who is unable to fill out this form independently, that is O.K. Feel free to use the form on your student's behalf. You might give the form to several members of the support team to fill out on behalf of the student, or perhaps do it as a group during a team meeting.

I like to fill out these sorts of forms in the presence of students I work with, doing so aloud, speaking the key phrases. Often students become engaged at some level. When this happens, choices can be given to the student as a way to elicit input. You do not need to know all the answers to fill out the form. Look at it as your best guess based on your observations. The important thing is to start. Once you have started, you can go back and enter new information as you discover it. Just having a form you have started to fill out helps you become aware of and, consequently, look for information pertinent to figuring our your student's sensory profile and resultant regulation strategies.

My Sensory Profile

The ISA Sensory Scan™

Welcome to the World of Sensory Integration

Since you are a person with an autism spectrum diagnosis or related condition, you, like so many of us with ASD, probably have challenges with the sensory world. Sometimes these challenges are difficult for us auties and aspies to identify, and quite often it's even harder for those around us to see or understand them.

Welcome to the world of sensory integration! The term "sensory integration" was coined by a remarkable woman named Jean Ayres. Dr. Ayres developed a theory that says our senses provide our brains with information about the environment around us, which in turn helps us respond to or organize our activities. For example, if you are indoors in a dark room and then step outside into a very sunny environment, you might find it difficult to adjust to the bright light. With time, your eyes might adapt to the change; however, some of us might need to take additional steps in order to be able to remain outdoors, such as putting on a hat or wearing a pair of sunglasses.

If you think about it, we are constantly informed by sensory experiences. You might have been told that there are five senses, but researchers have actually found that, in addition to the five traditional senses we often hear about (visual, oral [taste], olfactory [smell], tactile [touch], and auditory [hearing]), there are two additional senses that can be less obvious to us. They are called the vestibular and proprioceptive systems. The *vestibular system* involves the position of your head and gravity. It tells you whether you are moving, spinning, or upside down. The *proprioceptive system* involves your awareness of your body, or parts of your body, in space, including your awareness of the direction in which your body is moving and the force with which it is moving.

Many of us on the autism spectrum have challenges with sensory integration. In other words, we don't adjust easily to some environments. For example, we might perceive sounds or smells that don't seem to bother others. At times, they can be so challenging that they prevent us from being able to participate fully in school lessons, activities with our families, or in community events.

The good news is that once you know more about your sensory profile (your sensory needs and preferences), you can either prepare for difficult sensory situations or you can advocate for a modification in the environment. On the following page is a list of all seven sensory systems. See if you can fill in the missing information in the grid – what function the particular sensory system fulfills. Your teacher can assist you with any areas you don't understand completely.

From Paradiz, V. (2009). *The integrated self-advocacy ISA™ curriculum: A program for emerging self-advocates with autism spectrum and other conditions. Student workbook.* Shawnee Mission, KS: Autism Asperger Publishing Company; pp. 26-27. Reprinted with permission.

Sensory Diagram		
	Sensory System	**Function**
	Visual	
	Olfactory	
	Oral	
	Auditory	
	Tactile	
	Vestibular	
	Proprioceptive	

Self-Reflection

1. Are you aware of any sensory challenges you have? Loud noises? Background noise? Don't like being touched? Difficulty reading handouts? Trouble with smells, like perfume? Can't feel hot things or other types of pain? Challenge with fluorescent lighting?

2. Have you ever felt frustrated by something in the sensory environment at home, in the community, or at school? Give examples. How did you react to it?

3. If you could change one thing in this room in terms of how it affects your senses, what would it be?

The ISA Sensory Scan™

Using the Sensory Scan worksheet, scan a room or other environment in school, where you work, or where you live.

From Paradiz, V. (2009). *The integrated self-advocacy ISA™ curriculum: A program for emerging self-advocates with autism spectrum and other conditions. Student workbook.* Shawnee Mission, KS: Autism Asperger Publishing Company; p. 27. Reprinted with permission.

Internal Regulation

The ISA Sensory Scan™ Worksheet
Integrated Self-Advocacy ISA®

My Personal Information & Scan Location

Your name: _____   Date: _____

School/grade/program: _____

Which room or environment will you be scanning? _____

The Sensory Scan

1. **Auditory Scan:** Pay attention to **the sound** in this environment. Which of the following apply to you? Fill in as many details as you can in the Notes sections.

   ☐ Background noise is distracting
   Notes:

   ☐ Challenge with number or volume of voice(s)
   Notes:

   ☐ Sudden loud noises
   Notes:

   ☐ Other
   Notes:

2. **Visual Scan:** Pay attention to **what you see or how you see** in this environment. Which of the following apply to you? Fill in as many details as you can in the Notes sections.

   ☐ Light in room is too bright or too dim
   Notes:

   ☐ Angle of light is difficult (from above, below, etc.)
   Notes:

   ☐ Distracted by things hanging on the wall or in my peripheral vision
   Notes:

   ☐ Type of light is distracting or challenging
   Notes:

   ☐ Challenges reading in this environment
   Notes:

   ☐ Other
   Notes:

3. **Olfactory Scan (Smell):** Pay attention to the **smells** in this environment. Which of the following apply to you? Fill in as many details as you can in the Notes sections.

   ☐ Smell from objects is distracting, challenging
   Notes:

   ☐ Smell from person(s) is distracting, challenging
   Notes:

   ☐ The general smell of the room is difficult
   Notes:

   ☐ Other
   Notes:

4. **Tactile Scan (Touch/Feel):** Pay attention to **your reaction to touch or to the things or people you touch/feel** in this environment. Which of the following apply to you? Fill in as many details as you can in the Notes sections.

   ☐ Generally cannot tolerate others' touch
   Notes:

   ☐ Sometimes don't feel pain the way others do
   Notes:

   ☐ Challenges with how things or surfaces feel to the touch (sticky, wet, rough, etc.)
   Notes:

   ☐ Other
   Notes:

5. **Oral Scan:** Pay attention to **tastes or textures on your tongue** in this environment. Which of the following apply to you? Fill in as many details as you can in the Notes sections.

☐ Challenges with the texture or taste of certain foods
Notes:

☐ Challenges with mixed foods
Notes:

☐ Other/Notes:

6. **Vestibular Scan:** Pay attention to **how movement affects or doesn't affect you** in this environment. Which of the following apply to you? Fill in as many details as you can in the Notes sections.

☐ Cannot sit for long periods of time
Notes:

☐ Would like to spin in circles
Notes:

☐ Motion in vehicles is disruptive/makes me feel sick or confused
Notes:

☐ Other
Notes:

7. **Proprioceptive Scan:** Pay attention to your experience of **your body and the space around you.** Which of the following apply to you? Fill in as many details as you can in the notes sections.

☐ Easily bump into others or the walls
Notes:

☐ Need to rock, bounce, or press against other things or people
Notes:

☐ Trouble writing on paper (graphomotor)
Notes:

☐ Difficulty using stairs or walking down an incline
Notes:

☐ Cannot sit for long periods of time
Notes:

☐ Other
Notes:

My Top Three Environmental Needs: Choose up to three results from your Sensory Scan above. You will use these to develop an Advocacy Plan in your *Self-Advocacy Portfolio*.

1.

2.

3.

From Paradiz, V. (2009). *The integrated self-advocacy ISA™ curriculum: A program for emerging self-advocates with autism spectrum and other conditions. Student workbook.* Shawnee Mission, KS: Autism Asperger Publishing Company; pp. 30-31. Reprinted with permission.

Internal Regulation

Stephen Shore, an adult with ASD and a professional in the field, has come up with a great visual way to depict someone's sensory profile called The Sensory Graphic Equalizer. The results from the Sensory Scan Worksheet can be plotted on The Sensory Graphic Equalizer. This is a great tool to show students visually when you see signs that they are in need of a sensory break. For example, when a student starts covering his ears to block sounds, you can draw his attention to the fact that you are moving the hearing slider up. This could be immediately followed by presenting the student with his sensory break card, thus linking the too much sensory input to the solution of taking a break to get the sensory system regulated to a place more conducive to learning.

Feel free to use The Sensory Graphic Equalizer in a way that makes sense for you and your student. Some students may benefit from a paper diagram they mark with a pencil, whereas other students may need you to construct The Sensory Graphic Equalizer with movable sliders for each sense. Again, any constructing and use of this tool can be done in front of the student, talking it through as you go, eliciting participation when interest is piqued.

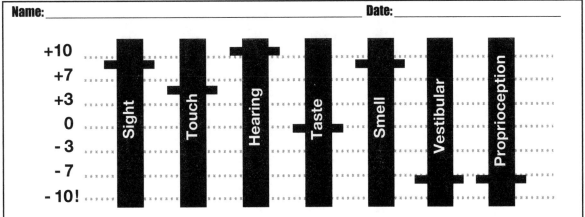

The Graphic Sensory Equalizer above depicts someone's sensory profile. Let's take a look at how this might play out in real life.

From Paradiz, V. (2009). *The integrated self-advocacy ISA™ curriculum: A program for emerging self-advocates with autism spectrum and other conditions. Student workbook.* Shawnee Mission, KS: Autism Asperger Publishing Company; p. 33. Reprinted with permission.

The Senses and Sensory Violations

The hypersensitive sense of sight is depicted in the example on the previous page with a slider up to almost positive 10 (+10). This person may be hypersensitive to fluorescent lights, perceiving them as a strobe light. It's also likely that this person has difficulties in the presence of down lights shining from above. Wearing a baseball cap may be helpful in such situations.

Touch is also hypersensitive for this person, but not quite as much as sight, resulting in difficulties in tolerating light touch on the skin (from others) or the feel of certain textures. Hearing is the most sensitive system on this person's equalizer, meaning that the person may perceive sounds such as the electricity in wires, or the buzzing of the ballasts in fluorescent lights may be intolerable. Note that the sense of taste in this case might be considered as "flat" or average, because the slider is at "0."

Moving on, low readings in the vestibular and proprioceptive realms indicate hypo-sensitivity, resulting in the need to seek sensory input. A person with sliders at this low end may like to spin herself around, seek deep pressure, and may consider a day on a roller coaster as great fun. Now it is time to fill out your own Sensory Graphic Equalizer. Using the situation where you are currently (the classroom, at home, etc.), simply indicate on the scale of -10 to +10 where you feel your sensory experience is.

My Sensory Equalizer

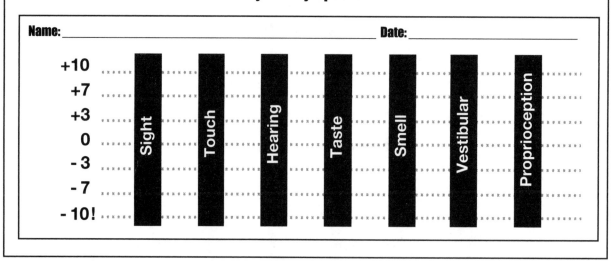

From Paradiz, V. (2009). *The integrated self-advocacy ISA™ curriculum: A program for emerging self-advocates with autism spectrum and other conditions. Student workbook.* Shawnee Mission, KS: Autism Asperger Publishing Company; p. 34. Reprinted with permission.

Instructions

1. Mark on the slider where you think your particular senses should be placed. If you are not sure, write your best guess in the form below.

2. In the form below, write something about each of your senses. If you are unable to think of anything at this time, make a check mark to remind you to come back later when something comes to mind.

1. Sight _____

    _____

    _____

2. Touch _____

    _____

    _____

3. Hearing _____

    _____

    _____

4. Taste _____

    _____

    _____

5. Smell _____

    _____

    _____

6. Vestibular _____

    _____

    _____

7. Proprioception _____

    _____

    _____

From Paradiz, V. (2009). *The integrated self-advocacy ISA™ curriculum: A program for emerging self-advocates with autism spectrum and other conditions. Student workbook.* Shawnee Mission, KS: Autism Asperger Publishing Company; p. 35. Reprinted with permission.

Tips for Encouraging Independence

To encourage independence involving sensory breaks, provide a clear and consistent process for how sensory breaks happen, along with clear beginnings and endings. For example,

1. Check schedule

2. Choose break item or activity (might use picture choice board or actual objects)

3. Set timer

4. Engage in activity until timer has run out

5. Put away item (or otherwise cease break)

6. Return to schedule to check what is next

The idea is to provide a concrete process for how to take a sensory break and highlight it with a visual. Some students have a book mark with a picture icon and/or words for each step of the process they find useful to enable them to eventually independently track the process and thus take their sensory breaks more independently.

Emotional Regulation

Just like the sensory system, our emotions often need conscious/intentional regulation. Learning how to regulate our emotions doesn't happen automatically, but with direct instruction, most people on the autism spectrum can and do learn to become better at regulating their emotions.

For individuals on the autism spectrum, triggered feelings become really big, really fast. And once it happens, it can take considerable time, and often concentrated effort, to get the really big feelings to come down to a more manageable level. Simply waiting it out – waiting until the big feelings dissipate – often isn't a practical option because this can take many hours and sometimes several days. Additionally, the big feelings can be overwhelming, and, if not brought down to a manageable level, can result in behavior that doesn't work well for all concerned.

Let me tell you a story from my own life about emotions getting triggered and becoming really big really fast and the resulting impact that has in my daily life.

Just like many people, I make a shopping list before going to the grocery store. My shopping list might include eggs, cheese, lettuce, apples, carrots, etc. Sometimes the grocery store is out of the brand of product I usually purchase. For example, when I notice the space for the bags of Cracker Barrel individually wrapped 2% sharp cheddar cheese is empty, I immediately get the same overwhelming, dreadful feeling in the pit of my stomach that I got when I first heard about the planes hitting the twin towers on 9-11.

Cognitively, I know that there is no comparison in level of horror between the two events. I also know that I enjoy many other varieties of cheese and that if I particularly want the Cracker Barrel 2% sharp cheddar cheese, I can get a brick of it and cut it into smaller pieces. Furthermore, I know that if I really do need that particular package of individually wrapped cheese, another grocery store will likely have it in stock.

But knowing all this is not helpful to me in the moment, because this is not a cognitive issue. Rather, it is an issue of **emotional disregulation**.

When my cheese is out of stock, my heart races, I feel faint, and become sweaty and panic-stricken in the pit of my stomach. It takes concerted effort to take slow, deep breaths while pushing my cart slowly and intentionally up and down the next three or four aisles of the store so I can finish my shopping. Sometimes I can get these too-big, too-fast feelings regulated so that my body can settle down. At other times I cannot and must leave the store without finishing my shopping.

No matter how much I would like to talk myself out of this experience, I haven't been able to figure out how to do so!

Learning to manage emotions doesn't happen automatically for most people with autism. One very helpful tool for students and the people who work with them is the *Incredible 5-Point Scale* (Buron & Curtis, 2003; Buron, 2007). This is a visual system that allows students to rank their feeling intensity from 1 through 5 and then sort out daily events according to the intensity number of big feelings each event incurs.

Fill in your own Stress Scale

Level	Makes me feel like this:	
5	This could make me lose control!!!!	
4	This can *really* upset me.	
3	This can make me feel nervous.	
2	This sometimes bothers me.	
1	This never bothers me.	

Buron, K. D. (2007). *A "5" could make me lose control! An activity-based method for evaluating and supporting highly anxious students*. Shawnee Mission, KS: Autism Asperger Publishing Company; p. 11. Reprinted with permission.

Using the scale, students and those who support them come up with strategies that help students' feelings come down from a high to a lower number, where they are better regulated and, the students, therefore, function better. Usually, different strategies are helpful as the intensity of the feeling increases. The strategies are individualized to particular students. While some strategies are generally helpful, such as slow, deep breathing and asking for help, it is important to determine the exact strategies your student finds helpful for each number 1-5 of feeling intensity.

Internal Regulation

Here is an example from a fourth-grade nonverbal student with classic autism, Stuart. The numbers represent the levels in the 5-point scale along with the smiley face icon Stuart assigned to each level. This is followed by the description of the sensory break to use at a particular level with Stuart's corresponding choice boards. Each choice board had actual photographs of the options listed. (Note: The scale must be read from the bottom up [1, 2, 3, etc.])

Level	Face	Sensory Break
5	☹	Add in hallway or OT room **reactive sensory break** to daily schedule (use choice board 2)
4	☹	Add in back of room **reactive sensory break** to daily schedule (choice board 4; i.e., wall push-ups, rocking chair, bean bag chair in reading corner)
3	😐	Add at desk **reactive sensory break** to daily schedule (choice board 3; i.e., desk push-ups, feet pushing against the therapy band attached to legs of desk, yellow clay squishing)
2	🙂	Follow daily schedule taking **proactive sensory breaks** as indicated with breaks in the hallway or in the OT room to allow Stuart bigger input from swing or walking (choice board 2; i.e., choice of brisk walk or swinging in OT room or on trampoline in OT room)
1	🙂	Follow daily schedule, taking **proactive sensory breaks** as indicated, with breaks being at Stuart's desk or in the classroom (choice board 1; i.e., water and oil toys, blue clay building, squeeze/pressure toys, kaleidoscope, mini etch-a-sketch, rocking chair, wall push-ups, beanbag chair in reading corner, desk push-ups, feet pushing against the therapy band attached to legs of desk, yellow clay squishing). Note: At this well-regulated stage, Stuart is able to choose from a wide variety of options.

Once the system has been constructed with strategies for each number (level) of feeling intensity, it is important that the visual be posted where the student can see it. It may sound elementary, but visuals that cannot be seen do not have much impact.

On the following page is the same chart with the choice boards presented so as to make it visual for the student.

Level	Face	Sensory Break		
5	☹			
4	☹			
3	😐			
2	☺			
1	☺			

For many students with classic autism, I have found that a visual that ties a solution strategy to an emotionally charged behavior is helpful. (Because this particular visual pertains to emotional regulation, it is discussed here. Chapter 4 offers a more complete discussion of the use of visual supports.) Many young children with classic autism are not able to understand the abstract concept of feeling intensity, but are more readily able to understand the idea of their behavior being on the line or crossing the line if this concept is made visual, as illustrated on page 61.

Internal Regulation

For students I support, it has worked well to have a simple visual with a white box on the bottom, a thick grey line in the middle, and a black box on the top, as illustrated below. A school picture of the child is placed in the white square when the child is well regulated.

Some children with very volatile emotions initially benefit from an adult using this visual to identify for them when their behavior has crossed the line. To do so, simply say "crossing the line" as you move the child's picture from the white square to the black square. All you are attempting to do at this initial stage is to pair the visual with the child's behavior so the child might begin to understand.

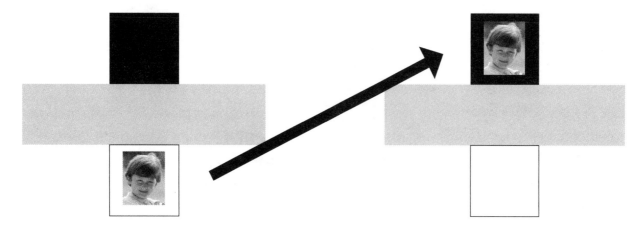

Activities that provide sensory regulation for a student also benefit the student in terms of emotional regulation. Therefore, a student who is afforded a mix of regularly scheduled (proactive) sensory breaks and sensory breaks in response to his changing needs (reactive) throughout the day will have much less intense emotional upsets from the physiological experience in the body that a quickly escalating intense emotion triggers.

To continue constructing this visual, place pictures of activities that provide sensory regulation for the student on the grey line. For some children, these pictures need to be covered (out of sight) until they are needed. If that is the case with your student, simply make the thick grey line twice the size needed horizontally so it can be folded over with the pictures between the fold.

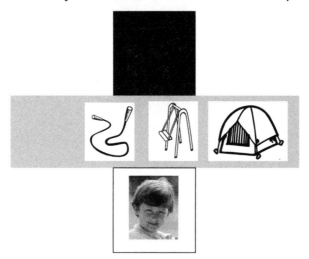

Then place a visual break card on the grey line along with pictures of the sensory-regulating activities. If your visual has a flap covering the pictures on the grey line, the break card may be placed either on top of the grey flap line or beneath the folds. Do whatever serves your student best.

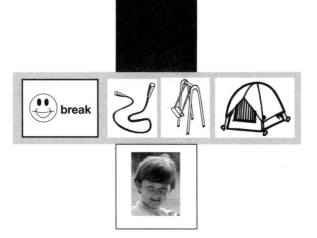

Internal Regulation

Initially, you will need to model how the system works. Each time a break time has arrived, move the child's picture to the break card, indicating she needs a break. Eventually, some students learn to do this independently, handing over the "I need a break" card to request a break.

Once the break card is ready, say "pick one" to the student. The idea is to present the student with picture choices that are regulating to her (based on a sensory assessment by an OT or on your knowledge of what activities are regulating for a particular student).

Some students are able to choose a picture; others need you to choose a picture for them. Do not make this an issue. Offer the choice, and if it is difficult for the student to choose, simply pick a picture. The important thing is to use the same process every time. Once students see the process implemented several times, some are able to choose independently when the "pick one" words are stated; other students put their picture on the break card, handing over both the break card and the icon representing which regulating activity they are choosing.

 For some students, it is important to eliminate the verbal prompt "pick one" as soon as possible by using the visual prompt only. This is especially important for students who easily become dependent on verbal prompting, and thus are unable to proceed until the prompt is offered.

If your student is like this, you may want to not even use the verbal prompt "pick one" but instead rely on the visual prompt of the regulating activities. To do this, you might run your finger under the visual icons as one does when using the pointer finger to visually track words one is reading and then choose which activity the student will be engaged in.

Some students find it useful to pick up the picture icon and place it in their picture schedule. Others simply point to their choice and engage in the activity without moving the picture icon. Make a thoughtful decision about the protocol that will best serve your student before you begin modeling the use of the system. Write down the exact steps you will follow, making yourself a cheat sheet of sorts. Then, follow your cheat sheet each time you use the visual system to ensure you are presenting the same sequence in the same manner to the student each time. This is how your student will come to learn the system and to use it.

If you vary how you use the visual or if you use lots of verbiage in the process, the use of the visual will not be clear to your student. The fewer words you speak, the more efficient it will be for your student. This will take some thoughtful planning on your part, especially if talking is part of how you naturally offer assistance to your student. **As students become disregulated, auditory input may become more overwhelming than usual. In addition, they are often not able to process the meaning of spoken words efficiently or effectively.**

Once the picture has been chosen, immediately set about engaging in the activity. Remember, the whole idea is to keep the sensory and the emotional systems well regulated so the student can be in a good place for learning to occur.

 This visual can be adapted to specific students as needed. Make certain that you provide only the picture choices that are available to the student at the time so that, regardless of the choice the student makes, it can happen. The grey line, in effect, becomes a choice board. Some support people put three choices on the grey line once the break card is put into use. This is especially important if not all regulating activities are available for the student to engage in at all times.

Use this visual system in a way that best supports your student by first teaching/showing him when his behavior is crossing the line and subsequently employing the picture solutions so as to better maintain regulation, knowing that sensory and emotional regulation activities have a huge overlap. For students with classic autism who are not able to talk about or cognitively understand their sensory or emotional disregulation, this visual system has proven to be helpful as a tool for both communication and regulation. For students who are able, it has become a tool for self-advocacy, as they use it to indicate they need a regulation opportunity.

Chapter 4
External Regulation

As emphasized throughout this book, neither internal nor external regulation happens easily or automatically for individuals with classic autism. We must bring deliberate and ongoing attention to these areas.

To continue the game board metaphor, finding the student's game piece is the internal regulation that needs to be in place. Then, once the game piece has been found, the external regulation allows the game piece to be placed on the "Go" square of the game board. It isn't until then that students are at their best, ready to engage in the game of life!

We will now turn our attention to this external regulation piece. As we have seen, a sensory diet is powerful for establishing a working internal organization. Visual schedules are just as powerful for establishing a working external organization. **When both a sensory diet and a visual schedule are in place, it is easier and more effective to evaluate the behavior that is left, if any.** I find that this is a lot easier and more efficient than starting with a functional behavior analysis (FBA) because so many behaviors fade away once the student is regulated.

In the following, we will discuss the nature of visual schedules, various types of such schedules, and how to effectively implement them.

What Exactly Is a Visual Schedule?

A visual schedule shows us how the world outside our body is organized. It allows us to see what's coming and to track the activities of the day. Everybody uses visuals. We all have calendars, daily planners, lesson plan books, etc. These are our visuals. When we drive down the road, we see all sorts of road signs and stop and go lights. Stores and places of business have names on them, men and women's restrooms are labeled, etc.

A visual schedule is essential for the student with classic autism because he doesn't arrive in the world knowing where to look to pick up the cues of what will happen next. Without any idea of what will happen in the world around him, life is very unpredictable and anxiety can be high.

What Does a Visual Schedule Look Like?

There is not one kind of picture schedule that is better than another. Many people end up wasting precious time because they deliberate over what sorts of pictures to use, what size to make the schedule, whether to hang it on the wall or make it portable, etc. The important thing is to start using a picture schedule. (Examples of picture schedules start on page 69.)

Most schools have Boardmaker (www.mayer-johnson.com), a software program with countless simple picture icons that they use when constructing a visual schedule. While it is handy to use Boardmaker, it is not a requirement. As an alternative, you can find and cut pictures out of magazines to represent activities students commonly engage in during the day.

Initially, you will need to determine what kinds of visual representation make sense to your student. Some students need to be taught that pictures represent real activities. If your student doesn't yet understand this, it is okay. It means that you will start with real items rather than pictures to represent the items.

It isn't practical to think of students progressing linearly along the continuum of visual representation from real objects to photographs of real objects, to simple line drawing to more complex line drawings, to icons or signs to words. Besides, it is supported by research evidence (Cadigan, Craig-Unkefer, Reichle, Sievers, & Gaylord, 2006/07). When working with students, look at what is currently being used and find out how effective it is. Then add other sorts of visual representations so that the student is exposed to many varieties along the continuum.

Some students show a definite preference in that they use only visuals with a particular visual representation. After the student has been exposed to various kinds of visual representations, try to let him choose the type of visual representation when constructing a new visual. In the age of computers, this is easy to do as all images can be stored on the computer. Besides being fun, this is a great way to interact with students, having them become part of constructing the visuals they need. After all, when they become adults, many will need to make their own visuals to support themselves to make daily life work optimally, allowing them to be their most competent selves as they live out their lives in the world.

One early childhood student who didn't find picture schedules helpful was readily able to understand when objects were used. His day started with looking at a book while the other students came in and got settled. Then, it was circle time. The teacher played the same music each day to gather the children to circle time. After circle time, the students rotated in small groups through three centers.

The way the teacher communicated what was going to happen to this particular student was by using objects to represent activities. The objects were set out at the end of a table – always in the same place, two objects at a time. When the student arrived in the morning, a book would be out and the tape recorder was set out next to the book in left-to-right order. The tape recorder played the song that gathered the children to circle time.

The student would get his book and sit in a beanbag chair, occupying himself looking at the book while the rest of the students made their way into the classroom. When the teacher was ready to invite the students to circle time, she would get an object from the first of the three centers the student would attend when it was center time. She would move the tape recorder over to the first spot (the place where the book had been sitting) and put the first center object (a box of crayons to represent the coloring center) next to the tape recorder. Then she would go to the beanbag chair and ask the student to turn on the tape recorder. It would take the student a minute or so to finish with the book and transition to the tape recorder. He would put his book on the bookshelf, go to the tape recorder, and turn it on. When doing so, he would see the box of crayons and thus know that the first center he would visit after circle time was the coloring center.

The teacher continued throughout the morning in this manner, always having two objects in left-to-right order on the table when the student returned to the table as each activity ended – the first object (on the left) to represent the next activity and the second object (on the right) to represent the activity that would follow.

After the student became familiar with this, a digital camera was used to take pictures of each of the objects. Then, for a time both the picture and the object were used and finally, just the pictures of the objects were used. Eventually, the student had a picture line-up of his entire morning activities; that is, a picture schedule.

Some schools use Boardmaker pictures to pair with real objects. I suggest using whatever is most conveniently at your disposal. If that doesn't seem to communicate the activity line-up to the student, then you may need to use something different – a different level of picture representation or perhaps a real object. Often when teachers search for the perfect pictures, several weeks can go by with no picture schedule put in place. This doesn't serve our students well.

Types of Schedules

Daily Schedule

MONDAY	
8:30	Swimming
9:20	Math
10:10	Science
11:00	Study Hall (sensory break)
11:50	Lunch
12:40	French
1:30	History
2:20	Homeroom (sensory break)

(Above) *Note.* For some students, it is necessary to indicate room number, materials to bring, etc.

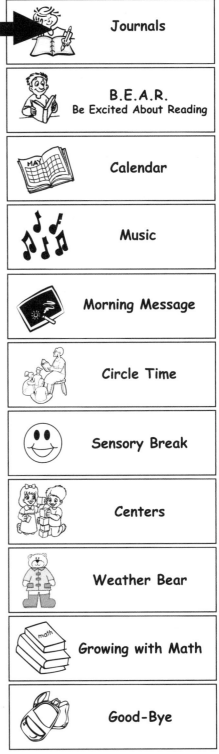

(Right) Vertical visual schedule.

Weekly Schedule

	MONDAY	TUESDAY	WEDNESDAY	THURSDAY	FRIDAY
8:30	Swimming	Swimming	Swimming	Swimming	Swimming
9:20	Math	Math	Math	Math	Math
10:10	Science	Science	Science	Science	Science
11:00	Study Hall (sensory break)	P.E. (sensory break)	P.E. (sensory break)	Study Hall (sensory break)	Study Hall (sensory break)
11:50	Lunch	Lunch	Lunch	Lunch	Lunch
12:40	French	Study Hall	Study Hall	French	French
1:30	History	History	History	History	History
2:20	Homeroom (sensory break)	Homeroom (sensory break)	Homeroom (sensory break)	Homeroom (sensory break)	Homeroom (sensory break)

In this sample weekly schedule, the student has color-coded his classes in chunks for locker stops during the day. When the student goes to his locker, he gets all class materials in a given color chunk as he will not be able to return to the locker until immediately prior to the next color chunk.

iPhone Application Schedule

NOTE: The following is a correction to the First/Then Schedule on page 71.

First

Then

WORKSHEET

1. _____
   _____
   _____

2. _____
   _____
   _____

3. _____
   _____
   _____

Monthly Schedule

OCTOBER						
S	M	T	W	T	F	S
1 🏠	2 🚌	3 🚌	4 🚌	5 🚌	6 🚌	7 🏠
8 🏠	9 🚌	10 🚌	11 🚌	12 🚌	13 🚌	14 🏠
15 🏠	16 🚌	17 🚌	18 🚌	19 🚌	20 🚌	21 🏠
22 🏠	23 🚌	24 🚌	25 🚌	26 🚌	27 🚌	28 🏠
29 🏠	30 🚌	31 🚌				

This schedule visually shows the child where she will be spending each day.

Monthly Cross-Off Calendar

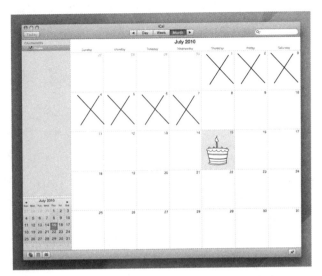

This child, whose birthday is July 15, has already started the countdown for the big day.

First/Then Schedule

Cross-Off Daily Schedule

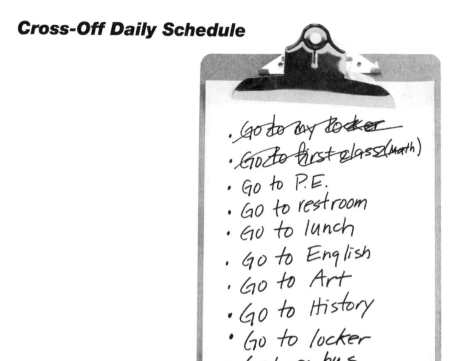

The idea here is to cross items off as they are completed.

Time and Place Choice Board Schedule Using Words

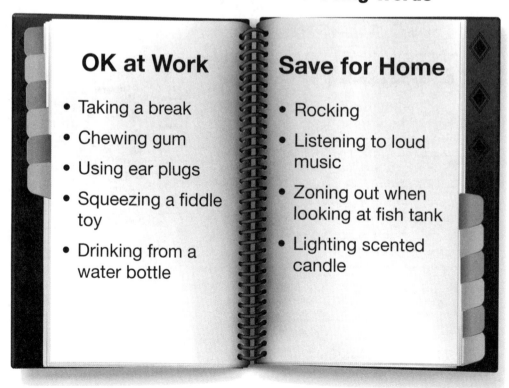

Time and Place Choice Board Schedule Using Pictures

Mini-Schedules

Some students need a more detailed road map of what will happen during a specific activity on their visual schedule. This might happen if a particular activity covers a long period of time, such as a language arts class that lasts 90 minutes, or if the student has difficulty tracking an activity. Also, if students have to do a less preferred activity, they may need a more detailed road map in terms of what will happen during the course of the activity. The mini-schedule allows students to clearly track the process of the undesired activity and see when it will end.

LANGUAGE ARTS MINI-SCHEDULE USING WORDS

Given the 90-minute language arts activity example, once the student arrives at the language arts picture on his schedule, you might visually show what will happen. For a reader, a written road map may suffice. Here is an example of a mini-schedule for this activity. The student puts a checkmark next to each activity as it is completed.

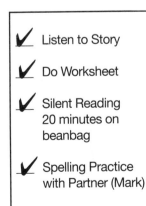

✔ Listen to Story

✔ Do Worksheet

✔ Silent Reading 20 minutes on beanbag

✔ Spelling Practice with Partner (Mark)

LANGUAGE ARTS MINI-SCHEDULE PAIRING VISUALS WITH WORDS

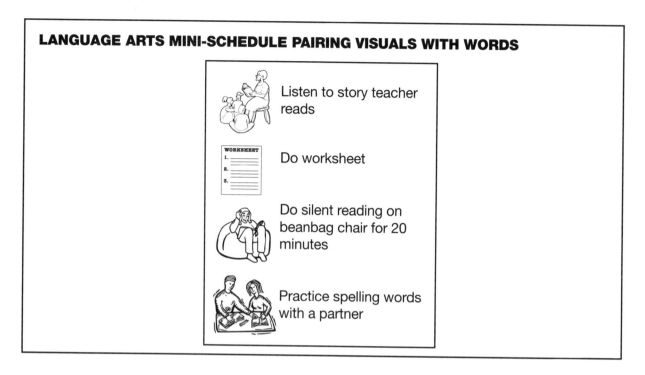

How Is a Visual Schedule Used?

For the student to get the most out of a visual schedule, it is best if the schedule is interactive. Imagine "living by the schedule," meaning that nothing can change without consulting the schedule. Initially, this is important for students who have very disorganized neurologies. Living by the schedule means that when an activity is finished, the picture representing that activity is removed and put in an "all-done" place. It is best if the student does this himself, so he can track what activity is finished, see what is coming next and thus see how the day is organized.

If your student doesn't participate initially, that is okay. Just draw his attention to it in a fun manner, using hand over hand to assist him in removing the all-done picture and putting it in the all-done place. Then direct his attention to what is next on the picture schedule.

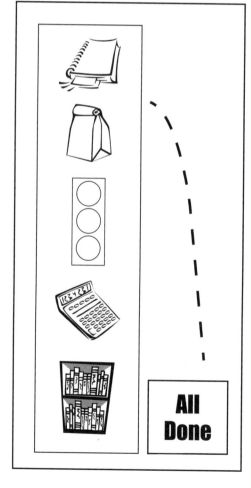

External Regulation

Many students benefit from using the same routine each time one activity is over and a new activity will begin. For students who have difficulty transitioning from one activity to another, using a picture schedule in the same interactive way for each transition goes a long way in supporting them in that it provides the very same transition routine each time the activity changes. Many teachers simply say, "Check your schedule" to signal when it is time for one activity to end and another to begin. Those words serve to initiate the transition routine which the student has learned to complete once initiated without further prompting.

When getting your student to use a schedule, whether it is a schedule with activities represented by real objects or one where activities are represented by pictures, it is important to be mindful of the prompts you put in for the student.

Before introducing anything new, think through how you want the student to ultimately engage in the activity.

- **Do you want the student to start only after you verbally prompt him?** For example, when a student puts a picture from his schedule into the "all-done" pocket, if you want him to be in the habit of waiting to start the next subject, you would teach him to only start after you prompt him saying something like, "Look what's next." Some teachers do this because they need to check over work the student just completed before wanting him to move on to the next subject or task on the schedule, or they may need to get materials for the student to use in the next subject or task.

- **Do you want one prompt to initiate a whole sequence?** It is most expedient to use one prompt such as "Get ready for the bus" to initiate the chain of events that is to occur when getting ready for the bus. Initially, the student may not know what getting ready for the bus entails. What often happens is that someone prompts the student each step of the way so as to offer support and to keep the student on track to ensure he is out the door to the bus on time. As a result, some students inadvertently learn to wait for the prompt each step of the way. To avoid this, it is helpful to provide a mini-schedule of pictures to show each step in getting ready for the bus. Then you can use one verbal prompt "Get ready for the bus" and use visuals for the student to track the process. Remember NOT to insert verbal prompts as you teach the student to follow the mini-schedule.

At the same time, when students are learning to follow the sequence of steps, you may need to repeatedly draw their attention to the visual. One way of doing this without speaking – and inadvertently creating a prompt – is to take the student's finger, put it on the beginning of the picture sequence, and then when he is looking, move his finger through the pictures that represent steps he has already completed, stopping at the picture showing where he is in the sequence. This designates what he is to do next.

It may take several days or weeks for the student to learn this, but once learned, it will be a lifelong skill as we need to "get ready" for countless things and situations. There can be visuals for the process of getting ready for several different things, such as getting ready for the day (self-care, getting dressed), getting ready for school (school clothes, lunch, backpack, jacket), and getting ready for bed (pajamas, brush teeth, story book). Adults get ready for work, for taking the car in for an oil change, for grocery shopping, etc. The fact is, we all "get ready" for many reoccurring events. All we are doing for our students is making that process visual, teaching it to them, and setting them up from the outset to be able to accomplish the entire process independently when we tell them, in this case, "Get ready for the bus."

- **Do you want the student to need a prompt each step of the way?** Occasionally you may want the student to wait for a prompt for each step of the way, such as on a field trip to a new place where you may not know exactly what will happen when. It then becomes helpful to the student to know that he can count on your prompt each step of the way. At the same time, it is helpful for you to know that the student will not do anything new until you prompt him to do so.

However, in most everyday situations it is not helpful for our students to need to be prompted each step of the way. Most everyday situations are repeated over and over, time after time. Neurotypical students learn from repeated routine that when the teacher says, "Time for math," she expects students to have their math book, math notebook, and pencil on their desk with everything else put away. However, our students with classic autism often need to be taught the routine directly as they do not pick up on routines in the same way neurotypical students learn them.

It is natural for us to verbally prompt each step of the process and that is what is helpful and what works for most students. In fact, it works so well that we don't even realize when we are doing it. Only when we prompt each step over and over more times than typically necessary for most students do we become frustrated. Verbally prompting each step of a sequence isn't an expedient way for many students with classic autism to learn routines. In fact, this often results in the teacher exasperatedly exclaiming, "He is sooooo prompt dependent!" **Just remember that for every prompt-dependent student, there has been a prompt-dependent teacher – rarely someone who set out to intentionally teach prompt dependency, but who nevertheless has taught his student well!**

Often, educational assistants work with students with ASD. Since they usually work with only one student, they end up talking a lot, which can translate into them using continuous verbal prompting in their well-intentioned attempt to be helpful to the student. Unfortunately, many students learn that the way to do any activity is to wait for the prompt each step of the way. In the end, they may not be able to use their picture schedule unless the teacher or assistant talks them through each and every step at every transition from one activity to the next.

To avoid such counterproductive outcomes, it is important to think carefully of the prompts up-front, only putting in what is necessary rather than all of a sudden realizing that your student is not able to use his picture schedule unless you are prompting him each step of the way. **It can be difficult to fade prompts, so it is best not to incorporate them in the first place.**

As students become more regulated, they may move through several activities on their visual schedule, and then all of a sudden you realize the visual schedule hasn't been changed along the way. That is okay. When it is time to transition to a new activity and the student goes to use the schedule, have him remove each schedule picture that is all done and put it in the all-done place.

For example, if the snack picture was not removed after snack, math followed and now you are finished with math, simply indicate that snack is all done, moving the snack picture. Then do the same with math, similarly moving the math picture. Have the student remove each picture in sequence, allowing him to accomplish the established transition routine for each picture. At any time when the student notices that the picture schedule is not correct because he has not moved a picture when the activity was finished, have him fix it right away.

Do not try to sneak the snack picture off to make the schedule look accurate! Well-intentioned people sometimes do this, trying to be helpful, but your student, who is likely more visual than you are, will know the snack picture disappeared.

The power of a visual schedule for a student with classic autism is that it organizes the world on the other side of his skin. If the student is not in charge of changing the schedule, or at least sees each time the visual schedule is changed, the power is lessened, and for some, it is lost altogether. The student needs to be able to count on the visual schedule. Thus, if the visual schedule arbitrarily loses pictures or gets changed around without him witnessing it, its power becomes watered down.

What if Things Change as the Day Goes Along?

Inevitably, the activities of the day sometimes change from what the student was told and, therefore, expects. The way to best deal with this in terms of the visual schedule is to have a change card to visually show the student that there will be a change. Then, after your student has seen the change card on his schedule – and while he is watching – you can make the necessary changes showing him how the change will make his schedule look.

For example, you might say, "Today we are having a change. We won't have social studies. We will have an assembly instead," while making this change with the pictures. If you don't have an assembly picture, that is okay. Just use the change card. Some teachers have a special symbol such as a star or a dinosaur they use for any sort of special activity. If the child has a particular interest such as dinosaurs, this can work well in terms of helping her accept the change because it is paired with a picture of something she finds interesting or comforting.

While you are saying the words to tell about the change, pair your words with the actions matching your words. For example,

When you say:	**Do this:**
"Today we are having a change."	Point to the change card.
"We won't have social studies."	Remove the social studies picture.
"We will have an assembly instead."	Put in the assembly picture – or use change card.

Some students interact less with their visual schedules as they become more organized, but this does not mean that they no longer need their visual schedules.

Everybody uses visuals. We all have calendars, daily planners, lesson plan books, etc. Just because we don't always look at each visual doesn't mean it is time to remove it or pack it away! Some of the power of these visuals comes from the fact that we know we can count on them being there whenever we need them.

For example, we don't always look at the speed limit signs as we drive around town, but we know we can whenever we need to know the speed limit. Imagine how nerve-wracking if would be if you could not count on which days speed limit signs would be available and which days they would arbitrarily be removed. This may be likened to our students' experience when we remove visual supports because they don't appear to be using them any more!

Visuals lose their power when we cannot see them! In addition, when we cannot see a visual that we need to see, our anxiety tends to escalate. Further, if we don't use the visual schedule each day, on days where changes occur, we won't have a good way to show it. It doesn't work well to wait until students are having trouble to pull out the visual schedule.

Again, imagine yourself driving in an unfamiliar section of town trying to find a new place of business. All the street signs, speed limit signs, and names of the places of business have been removed. A police car is on each block to chase after speeders. You have been issued a few tickets. Your anxiety is high, because you are late, and you still don't have a clue which street to turn down. And even if you arbitrarily choose the correct, un-labeled street, you will have to also have the good fortune to choose the correct place of business from all the unlabeled businesses on the street. If all of a sudden a few visuals pop up, they may be helpful, but because you are now anxious, they are not as helpful as they would have been had they never been removed in the first place. In addition, once you have had this experience, you now have no idea if and when the signs might disappear again. Thus, the power of the visuals has been watered down for you.

It is crucial for most students with classic autism to have their visuals available at all times, so they can be counted on and, in turn, provide the external regulation that is needed. Don't we all function much better when anxiety is low because needed visuals are in place?

Are Sensory Breaks Necessary When Visuals Are Used?

Often after a student becomes calmer and is participating in the school day more smoothly, staff members start taking away sensory breaks. In fact, when sensory breaks have been taken away, most staff are proud initially to report that their student no longer needs them.

Be careful not to remove too many breaks too quickly. Remember the purpose of a break is to provide sensory regulation to a system that does not regulate itself. Needs do change over time, but even as an adult, I have to consciously take time to regulate myself each day, whether I look like I need it or not! **No matter how well regulated we become, we need to actively maintain that regulation each day.**

For How Long Should a Visual Schedule Be Used?
(After all, we don't want our students to become dependent on them ...)
Many concerned teachers want to wean their students off their visual schedules so they look more like other students and because they don't want students to become dependent on visuals. This may make sense intuitively, but the fact is that we are all dependent on visuals. I like to think that our students with autism are just more advanced than typical students in that they use a daily planner way ahead of the time typical students are likely to start using one.

Instead of thinking of weaning students off their visual schedules, we might think ahead, looking at the bigger picture. As students advance from one grade to the next, their visual schedules can change so as to look most like the daily planner other students are using.

The primary reason for the visual schedule is to support a neurology that doesn't automatically sort out what is going on externally. So, the way the schedule looks must first and foremost provide the support the student needs.

Does the Student Who Reads Need a Picture Schedule?

Sometimes teachers do not want to use pictures for a student who can read. Know that words are visuals! Sometimes the shape of the word is what is helpful, and at other times meaning is gleaned from actually reading the word and pulling up the understanding that goes with the written word. Some middle and high school students on the autism spectrum need to hang onto their class schedules and use them each day, whereas most other students don't use them after the first few days or weeks of the new school year.

Another important factor to keep in mind is that for those who think in pictures, written and spoken language is typically less salient than pictures. Practically speaking, this might mean that some of your students who are new readers need the words paired with the pictures for a while. Some teachers put words on the visual schedule and put the picture on the back for students who don't want pictures, but still need to be able to sneak a peek when they are stressed.

 For me, most of the time words on a to do-list or a schedule work fine. However, when I am disregulated, I don't always pick up meaning from words, even though I might still be able to use them.

The first meaning to fall out is from words I hear other people speak. Shortly after that, I am well able to read words, but the meaning of the words I read is lost. During this time, I still get the full meaning of pictures. My brain works in pictures. When stressed in any way, I automatically understand the world best in my primary language of pictures. In fact, all my words are translations of the pictures in my head.

Alternative Augmentative Communication Devices and Visual Schedules

Since many students with classic autism have limited verbal abilities or are nonverbal, they may have learned to use the Boardmaker pictures in the context of PECS (Picture Exchange Communication System; www.pecs.com; Frost & Bondy, 1994) or a natural aided language (NAL) board (Cafiero, 1998).

Some students who use alternative augmentative communication devices that use icons, including PECS, NAL, etc., when seeing the same picture icons used in the daily picture schedule treat them as pictures of communication. Thus, they may think they can throw away the math icon if they do not wish to participate in math and give you the snack icon whenever they would like to eat a snack. If this happens, celebrate the fact that your student likes to communicate with you! Also know there are simple remedies to this situation.

When students are familiar with PECS and you use the same picture icons in their visual schedules, you may need a way to show the difference between the icons intended to be handed over as requests and the non-negotiable picture schedule icons. There are several simple ways to do this, including …

1. Use colored paper to print the picture schedule icons on so the background is colored instead of white.

2. Copy the daily picture line-up so that it is all on one sheet of paper and then have the students cross off each activity as it is finished.

The visual schedule, in my opinion, remains the single most powerful external regulation tool. In addition, visual timers are a great way to provide visual support to show how long something will last. Again, our students don't automatically pick up social cues or may not have the necessary understanding or be able to track time on a clock. They often need visual support that provides a clear beginning and ending to tasks and activities.

Many natural things can be used to show a clear beginning and ending besides a visual timer, including …

1. Putting a specific number of flashcards on a student's desk to show how many he needs to do, or

2. Drawing a line under the last problem he needs to complete on a worksheet.

Tips for Encouraging Independence

1. Engage students in the process of using visual supports, supporting them to remove "all done" picture icons, crossing-off, or whatever their particular schedule requires.

2. If you are building the students' schedules each day for them, allow them to see you do so. Over time, engage their help, supporting them to do as much as possible in setting up their own visual schedule.

3. For most of our students, there are variations in each day of the week. Some classes are not held daily, and most of our students have special services such as speech, occupational and physical therapy, and so on. One easy solution to support independence in this situation is to make a photo copy of the schedule for each day of the week. Then, on Monday show your student the photo copy of the Monday schedule and use it to pull out the picture icon matches to his photo copied Monday schedule, placing them in same order, thus effectively copying from the photocopied Monday page to construct the student's actual Monday picture schedule with his picture schedule icons.

Some students set up their schedules at the beginning of each day. Others benefit from priming, or previewing, provided by setting up the next day's schedule at the end of the preceding day so it is ready for them when they arrive at school the following school day.

Conclusion

As students become more regulated, visual supports can be added along with more strategies to help them continue to sort out the world around them with all the various social expectations.

Students with classic autism must first be well regulated internally and externally by using the methods outlined in this book. Once regulated, all the various supports that have been found helpful to individuals on the spectrum can now be tried for the well-regulated student with classic autism. This book illustrated the small but necessary piece in daily life of "getting to Go": the two essential elements – internal and external regulation support.

A prescriptive sensory diet by an occupational therapist, combined with an interactive visual schedule used properly, will support internal and external regulation for the student with classic autism. As he becomes internally regulated, the student will be able to find his game piece, and the external visual schedule support will allow him to place his game piece on the "Go" square in the game of life. When this happens, you will be able to use the various other supports that work well with those with autism to support the student as he plays in his game of life.

Good luck, and get ready to have a lot of fun. Students with classic autism, in my opinion, are the most fun to support, love, and learn from as I play out my hand in my game of life. Welcome aboard!

References

Attwood, T. (2007). *The complete guide to Asperger's Syndrome.* London: Jessica Kingsley Publishers.

Aspy, R., & Grossman, B. G. (2007). *The Ziggurat model: A framework for designing comprehensive interventions for individuals with high-functioning autism and Asperger Syndrome.* Shawnee Mission, KS: Autism Asperger Publishing Company.

Brack, J. C. (2004). *Learn to move, move to learn: Sensorimotor early childhood activity themes.* Shawnee Mission, KS: Autism Asperger Publishing Company.

Brack, J. C. (2009). *Learn to move, moving up! Sensorimotor elementary-school activity themes.* Shawnee Mission, KS: Autism Asperger Publishing Company.

Buron, K. D. (2007). *A "5" could make me lose control.* Shawnee Mission, KS: Autism Asperger Publishing Company.

Buron, K. D., & Curtis, M. (2003). *The incredible 5-point scale: Assisting students with autism spectrum disorders in understanding social interactions and controlling their emotions.* Shawnee Mission, KS: Autism Asperger Publishing Company.

Cadigan, K., Craig-Unkefer, L., Reichle, J., Sievers, P., & Gaylord, V. (Eds.). (Fall/Winter 2006/07). *Impact: Feature Issue on Supporting Success in School and Beyond for Students with Autism Spectrum Disorders, 19*(3). [Minneapolis: University of Minnesota, Institute on Community Integration].

Cafiero, J. (1998). Communication power for individuals with autism. *Focus on Autism and Other Developmental Disabilities, 13*(2), 113-121.

Case-Smith, J., & Arbesman, M. (2008). Evidence-based review of interventions for autism used in or of relevance to occupational therapy for children with autism spectrum disorder. *Journal of Occupational Therapy, 62,* 416-429.

Donnellan, A. M., Hill, D. A., & Leary, M. R. (2010). Rethinking autism: Implications of sensory and movement differences. *Disability Studies Quarterly, 30,* 1.

Donnellan, A. M., Leary, M., & Robledo, J. (2006). I can't get started: Stress and the role of movement differences for individuals with the autism label. In G. Baron, J. Groden, G. Groden, & L. Lipsitt (Eds.), *Stress and coping in autism* (pp. 205-245). Oxford, UK: Oxford University Press.

Dunn, W. (1997). The impact of sensory processing abilities on the daily lives of young children and their families: A conceptual model. *Infants and Young Children, 9*(4), 23-25.

Dunn, W. (2008). Sensory processing: Identifying patterns and support strategies. In K. D. Buron & P. Wolfberg (Eds.), *Learners on the autism spectrum: Preparing highly qualified educators* (pp. 138-159). Shawnee Mission, KS: Autism Asperger Publishing Company.

Dziuk, M. A., Larson, J.C.G., Apostu, A., Mahone, E. M., Denckla, M. B., & Mostofsky, S. H. (2007). Dyspraxia in autism: association with motor, social, and communicative deficits. *Developmental Medicine & Child Neurology, 49*(10), 734-739.

Endow, J. (2009). *Outsmarting explosive behavior: A visual system of support and intervention for individuals with autism spectrum disorders.* Shawnee Mission, KS: Autism Asperger Publishing Company.

Fertel-Day, D., Bedell, G., & Hinojosa, J. (2001). Effects of a weighted vest on attention to task and self-stimulatory behaviors in preschoolers with pervasive developmental disorders. *American Journal of Occupational Therapy, 55,* 629-640.

Freitag, C. M., Kleser, C., Schneider, M., & von Gontard, A. (2007). Quantitative assessment of neuromotor function in adolescents with high functioning autism and Asperger Syndrome. *Journal of Autism and Developmental Disorders, 37*(5), 948-959.

Frost, L. A., & Bondy, A. (1994*). PECS: The picture exchange communication system.* Cherry Hill, NJ: Pyramid Educational Consultants.

Henry, S. A., & Myles, B. S. (2007). *The Comprehensive autism planning system (CAPS) for individuals with Asperger Syndrome, autism, and related disabilities: Integrating best practices throughout the student's day.* Shawnee Mission, KS: Autism Asperger Publishing Company.

References

Kazek, B., Huzarska, M., Grzybowska-Chlebowczyk, U., Kajor, M., Cuipinska-Kajor, M., Wos, H., & Marszal, E. (2010). Platelet and instrtinal 5-HT$_{2a}$ mRNA receptor in autistic spectrum disorders: Results of a pilot study. *Acta Neurobiologiae Experimentalis, 70,* 232-238.

Kerstein, L. H. (2008). *My sensory book: Working together to explore sensory issues and the big feelings they can cause: A workbook for parents, professionals, and children.* Shawnee Mission, KS: Autism Asperger Publishing Company.

Kluth, P. (2003). *"You're going to love this kid!" Teaching students with autism in the inclusive classroom.* Baltimore: Paul H. Brookes Publishing Company, Inc.

Koomar, J., Kranowitz, C., Szklut, S., Balzer-Martin, L., Haber, E., & Sava, D. I. (2007). *Answers to questions teachers ask about sensory integration.* Arlington, TX: Future Horizons, Inc.

Kranowitz, C. (1998). *The out-of-sync child: Recognizing and coping with sensory integration dysfunction.* New York: Skylight Press and Carol Stock Kranowitz.

Lavoie, R. D. (1994). *Learning disabilities and social skills with Richard Lavoie: Last one picked ... First one picked on* [Video and Teacher's Guide]. (Available from PBS Video, 1320 Braddock Place, Alexandria, VA 22314-1698)

Leary, M. R., & Hill, D. A. (1996). Moving on: Autism and movement disturbance. *Intellectual and Developmental Disabilities, 34,* 42-48.

Maurer, R., & Damasio, A. (1982). Childhood autism from the point of view of behavioral neurology. *Journal of Autism and Developmental Disorders, 12,* 195-205.

Myles, B. S., Adreon, D., & Gitlitz, D. (2006). *Simple strategies that work! Helpful hints for all educators of students with Asperger Syndrome, high-functioning autism, and related disabilities.* Shawnee Mission, KS: Autism Asperger Publishing Company.

Myles, B. S., Cook, K., Miller, N. E., Rinner, L., & Robbins, L. A. (2000). *Asperger Syndrome and sensory issues: Practical solutions for making sense of the world.* Shawnee Mission, KS: Autism Asperger Publishing Company.

National Center for Clinical Infant Programs/Zero to Three. (1994). *Diagnostic classification of mental health and developmental disorders of infancy and early childhood.* Arlington, VA: Author.

Staples, K., & Reid, G. (2009). Fundamental movement skills and autism spectrum disorders. *Journal of Autism and Developmental Disorders,* 1-9.

Valicenti-McDermott, M. D., McVicar, K., Cohen, H.J., et al. (2008 Gastrointestinal symptoms in children with an autism spectrum disorder and language regression. *Pediatric Neurology, 39*, 392–398.

VandenBerg, N. (2001). The use of a weighted vest to increase on-task behavior in children with attention difficulties. *American Journal of Occupational Therapy, 55*(6), 621-628.

Wilbarger, P. (1995, June). The sensory diet: Activity programs based on sensory processing theory. *Sensory Integration Special Interest Section Newsletter, 18*, 1-4.

Williams, M. W., & Shellenberger, S. (1996). *How does your engine run? A leader's guide to the alert program for self-regulation.* Albuquerque, NM: Therapy Works

www.mayer-johnson.com/boardmaker

www.pecs.com

www.timetimer.com

Recommended Resources

Bellini, S. (2008). *Building social relationships: A systematic approach to teaching social interaction skills to children and adolescents with autism spectrum disorders and other social difficulties.* Shawnee Mission, KS: Autism Asperger Publishing Co.

This book addresses the need for social programming for children and adolescents with ASD by providing a comprehensive model for how to organize and make sense of the myriad social skills strategies and resources currently available to parents and professionals. It is not meant to replace other resources or strategies, but synthesize them into one comprehensive program.

Buron, K. D. (2005). *When my worries get too big.* Shawnee Mission, KS: Autism Asperger Publishing Company.

The thought of "losing control" can cause major problems for children who live with anxiety. This helpful tool gives young children an opportunity to explore their own feelings with parents or teachers as they react to events in their daily lives. Engaging and easy to read, this illustrated children's book is filled with opportunities for children to participate in developing their own self-calming strategies. Children who use the simple strategies in this charming book, illustrated by the author, will find themselves relaxed and ready to focus on work – or play!

Endow, J. (2006). *Making lemonade: Hints for autism's helpers.* Cambridge, WI: Cambridge Book Review Press.

Fascinating storytelling and classic elements of poetry combine to allow the reader into the world of autism. Faced with a lifetime of "lemons," Judy decided years ago that rather than (a) throwing them out or (b) letting them rot and then throwing them out, she would (c) make lemonade – capitalizing on her strengths and talents. Each poem in the collection invites us to focus on one of Judy's lemons, such as sensory lemons, her school days, etc. By choosing her words simply and sparingly, the author trusts us to fill in the spaces with our own experience, encouraging us to accept our own lemons and make our own lemonade.

Endow, J. (2009). *Paper words: Discovering and living with my autism.* Shawnee Mission, KS: Autism Asperger Publishing Company.

In this intensely personal book, readers are swept up into a fast-paced journey of how author Judy Endow noticed her differences early on, how she eventually discovered her autism, and how she embraces life autistically.

Espin, R. (2003). *Amazingly ... Alphie! Understanding and accepting different ways of being.* Shawnee Mission, KS: Autism Asperger Publishing Co. (children's book)

A story book that fosters tolerance and acceptance while celebrating differences. Readers are introduced to Alphie, a computer that is "wired differently" and has trouble fitting in and performing successfully in the world around him until he learns about his differences and how to use his abilities to their fullest.

Hodgdon, L. A. (1996). *Visual strategies for improving communication.* Troy, MI: Quirk-Roberts Publishing.

One of the most comprehensive books to explain the use of visual strategies to improve communication for students with autism spectrum disorders and students who experience moderate to severe communication impairments. It contains easy-to-use techniques and strategies that will help these students participate more effectively in social interactions and life routines.

Hodgdon, L. A. (1999). *Visual strategies for solving behavior problems in autism.* Troy, MI: QuirkRoberts Publishing.

A book showing very practical approaches to behavior management for students with autism spectrum disorders. Continuing the approach of supporting communication with visual strategies, the book is packed with problem-solving techniques. You will find lots of examples of visual tools and strategies that have been used effectively to solve behavior problems.

Hudson, J., & Myles, B. S. (2007). *Starting points: The basics of understanding and supporting children and youth with Asperger Syndrome.* Shawnee Mission, KS: Autism Asperger Publishing Company.

Starting from the premise that no two individuals with Asperger Syndrome are the same, Hudson and Myles provide a global perspective of how the core characteristics of AS may appear separately and/or simultaneously, and how they may manifest themselves in a variety of situations. Each characteristic is then paired with a brief explanation, followed by a series of bulleted interventions. Interventions include strategies and visual supports that help children on the spectrum who have difficulty with abstract concepts and thoughts, difficulty understanding and regulating emotions, difficulty recognizing, interpreting, and empathizing with the emotions of others and much more.

Recommended Resources

Kluth, P., & Schwarz, P. (2008). *"Just give him the whale" – 20 ways to use fascinations, areas of expertise, and strengths to support students with autism.* Baltimore: Paul H. Brookes Publishing Co.

This book shows how to use students' fascinations in a positive way that supports their learning.

McGinnity, K., & Negri, N. (2005). *Walk awhile in my autism: A manual of sensitivity presentations to promote understanding of people on the autism spectrum.* Cambridge, WI: Cambridge Book Review Press.

This book allows readers of all ages and sizes to "try on" a bit of an experience of what it is like to live in a body with autism. An experience is often worth more than any amount of explanation!

Mitchell, L. (1999). *Different just like me.* Watertown, MA: Charlesbridge Publishing.

A children's story book explaining differences.

Moyer, S. A. (2009). *The ECLIPSE model—Teaching self-regulation, executive function, attribution, and sensory awareness to students with Asperger Syndrome, high-functioning autism, and related disorders.* Shawnee Mission, KS: Autism Asperger Publishing Company.

The ECLIPSE Model targets the skills needed to improve social competence, such as executive functioning, theory of mind, causal attribution, processing speed and working memory. Without effective use of these skills on a regular basis, development of other areas of functioning – academic, adaptive, social and vocational skills – will be inhibited.

Myles, B. S., Cook, K., Miller, N. E., Rinner, L., & Robbins, L. A. (2000). *Asperger Syndrome and sensory issues: Practical solutions for making sense of the world.* Shawnee Mission, KS: Autism Asperger Publishing Company.

Asperger Syndrome and Sensory Issues attempts to explain how many children with Asperger Syndrome relate to the world through their senses. Chapter 1 is an overview of sensory integration terminology and a discussion of how the sensory systems impact behavior. Chapter 2 takes an in-depth look at sensory issues associated with AS. Chapter 3 introduces assessment tools that can assist you in pinpointing sensory characteristics. Chapter 4 offers a series of intervention strategies. Chapter 5 presents a case study outlining the sensory assessment of and subsequent programming for a child with AS.

Udvari-Solner, A., & Kluth, P. (2008). *Joyful learning: active and collaborative learning in inclusive classrooms.* Thousand Oaks, CA: Corwin Press.

This book shows how to make classroom inclusion work, particularly for students with autism spectrum disorders.

Williams, D. (1996). *Autism: An inside-out approach.* Philadelphia: Jessica Kingsley Publishers.

> Focusing on three faces of autism – problems of connection, problems of tolerance, and problems of control – this book goes beyond the label to the systems and mechanics of what is going on. It gives detailed suggestions for strategies to reduce these burdens in a way that takes into account of the experience of autism from the inside.

Williams, D. (1998). *Autism and sensing: The unlost instinct*. Philadelphia: Jessica Kingsley Publishers.

> This book, written by a person diagnosed with autism, emphasizes the importance of the system of sensing in understanding more classically autistic individuals.

www.autism-society.org

www.coultervideo.com

www.ideapartnership.org/index.php?option=com_content&view=article&id=1493

www.ocali.org/

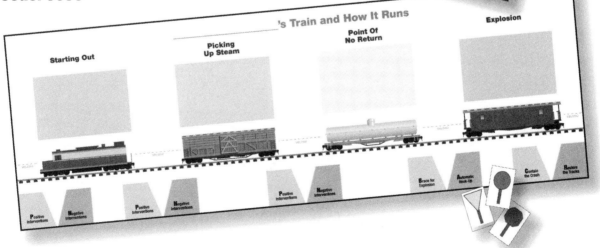

PUBLISHING

P.O. Box 23173
Overland Park, Kansas 66283-0173
www.asperger.net